Come Back Here, Crocodile

Donna Alvermann
Connie A. Bridge
Barbara A. Schmidt
Lyndon W. Searfoss
Peter Winograd

D.C. Heath and Company
HEATH Lexington, Massachusetts   Toronto, Ontario

Acknowledgments

Grateful acknowledgment is made for permission to reprint the following copyrighted material.

Allen, Marjorie N. **One, Two, Three-Ah-Choo!** excerpt adapted by permission of Coward, McCann & Geoghegan from *One, Two, Three-Ah-Choo!* by Marjorie N. Allen, text copyright © 1980 by Marjorie N. Allen.

Anderson, Lonzo. Adapted from **Izzard.** Copyright © 1973 by John Lonzo Anderson. Reprinted with the permission of Charles Scribner's Sons.

Andrews, F. Emerson. **Nobody Comes to Dinner** is adapted by permission of Little, Brown and Company. Text copyright © 1976 by F. Emerson Andrews.

Brenner, Barbara. Adaptation from **Wagon Wheels**, by Barbara Brenner. Text copyright © 1978 by Barbara Brenner. Reprinted by permission of Harper & Row, Publishers, Inc.

Brown, Marc. **Arthur's Eyes,** copyright © 1979 by Marc Brown. Reprinted by permission of Little, Brown and Company, in association with the Atlantic Monthly Press.

Cooper, Elizabeth K. **The Fish From Japan,** copyright © 1969 by Elizabeth K. Cooper, is adapted and reprinted by permission of Harcourt Brace Jovanovich, Inc.

Fisher, Aileen. "**Butterfly Wings,**" from *In the Woods, in the Meadow, in the Sky.* Copyright © 1965 by Aileen Fisher. Reprinted by permission of Charles Scribner's Sons.

Gardner, John. "**The Crab,**" from *A Child's Bestiary,* by John Gardner. Copyright © 1977 by Boskydell Artists, Ltd. Reprinted by permission of Alfred A. Knopf, Inc.

Hall, Judy. "**Make Your Own Instruments,**" from *Cobblestone*'s October 1983 issue "Jazz." Copyright © 1983 by Cobblestone Publishing, Inc., Peterboro, NH 03458. Reprinted by permission of the publisher.

Hillert, Margaret. "**Just Me**" is reprinted by permission.

Hornblow, Leonora, and Arthur Hornblow. From **Fish Do the Strangest Things,** by Leonora and Arthur Hornblow. Copyright © 1966 by Random House, Inc. Reprinted by permission of the publisher.

Horvath, Betty. **Jasper Makes Music.** Copyright © 1967 by Betty Horvath, reprinted by permission of Franklin Watts, Inc.

Jones, Betty Millsaps. "**A Perfect Ten,**" adapted by permission of Random House, Inc., from *Wonder Women of Sports,* by Betty Millsaps Jones. Copyright © 1981 by Random House, Inc. Reprinted by permisssion of the publisher.

Kennedy, X.J. "**Sea Horse and Sawhorse,**" from *One Winter Night in August.* Reprinted by permisssion of Curtis Brown, Ltd., copyright © 1975 by X.J. Kennedy.

Kent, Jack. Adaptation from the book **The Caterpillar and the Polliwog,** by Jack Kent, copyright © 1982 by Jack Kent. Used by permission of the publisher, Prentice-Hall, Inc., Englewood Cliffs, N.J.

Livingston, Myra Cohn. "**Reflection,**" from *A Song I Sang to You,* by Myra Cohn Livingston. Copyright © 1957, 1958, 1967, 1969, 1984, by Myra Cohn Livingston. All rights reserved. Reprinted by permission of Marian Reiner for the Author.

Lonsdale, Mary. "**Wheels Are Turning**" is reprinted by permission of the Author.

Maestro, Giulio. "**Shark,**" from *Riddle Romp* by Giulio Maestro. Copyright © 1985 by Giulio Maestro. Reprinted by permission of Clarion Books/Ticknor & Fields, a Houghton Mifflin Company.

Marshall, Edward. "**Fox on Wheels,**" adapted from *Fox on Wheels,* by Edward Marshall. Text copyright © 1983 by Edward Marshall. Reprinted by permission of the publisher, Dial Books for Young Readers.

McCord, David. "**Song of the Train,**" from *One at a Time,* copyright 1952, is reprinted by permission of the Author and Little, Brown and Company.

Peterson, Esther Allen. **Penelope Gets Wheels,** reprinted from *Penelope Gets Wheels,* by Esther Allen Peterson. Copyright © 1981 by Crown Publishers, Inc. Used by permission of Crown Publishers, Inc.

Poe, Maurice. "**Elephant for Sale,**" from *Willie MacGurkle and Friends.* Copyright © 1987 by Curriculum Associates, Inc. Reprinted by permission of Curriculum Associates, Inc.

Rabe, Berniece. **The Balancing Girl.** Adaptation of *The Balancing Girl,* by Berniece Rabe. Text copyright © 1981 by Berniece Rabe. Reprinted by permission of the publisher, E.P. Dutton, a division of NAL Penguin, Inc.

(Continued on page 287)

Table of Contents

Rolling Along

Sounds Fishy!

Pick a Pet

Musicmakers

Balancing Act

What Are Friends For?

Be Yourself

Tricksters

Come Back Here, Crocodile

Wheels are turning, turning, turning,
Wheels are turning all around,
Rolling, rolling always rolling,
Wheels are rolling through the town.

WHEELS ARE TURNING *by Mary Lonsdale*

Rolling Along

FOX ON WHEELS

by Edward Marshall

One Saturday morning Fox ate breakfast
in a hurry.

"I'm off to meet the gang!" he said.

"Hold your horses," said Mom.

"But we're going to have a bike race!"
said Fox.

"You can race later," said Mom. "I need some help around here."

"Doing what?" said Fox.

"Take your choice," said Mom. "You can look after Louise, or you can go shopping."

Fox looked at Louise. "Too much trouble," he said. "I'll shop."

"Here is the list," said Mom.

"This will take *all day!*" said Fox.

"Then you must hurry," said Mom. "And don't forget the tuna fish for Louise's lunch."

At the market Fox ran into the gang.
They had to shop too.

"We'll just have to race later," said Fox.

"Too bad," said Dexter.

"I have an idea," said Carmen. "Why don't we race right now?"

"Great idea!" said her friends.

"Let's race from one end of the store to the other!" said Fox.

"Fine!" said the gang.

"On your mark, get set, go!" cried Fox.

And the race was on!

Dexter pulled out ahead. "Gangway!" he cried. Suddenly a wheel fell off his cart. "Nuts!" said Dexter. "I'm out of the race!"

"Beep, beep!" cried Carmen.

Other shoppers ran for their lives.

Carmen was about to win. But just then her cart crashed into a bin of pickles.

"Oh, my!" said Carmen.

"Hooray!" cried Fox. "I won, I won!"

But some of the shoppers had angry words for Mr. Sloan.

"Shopping here is *dangerous!*" said nice Mrs. O'Hara.

"It won't happen again," said Mr. Sloan.

When Fox got home, his mom was on the phone.

"Oh, really?" said Mom. "He didn't! He *did?* Well, it won't happen again!"

Then she hung up the phone.

"I hear you're the fastest fox on wheels," said Mom.

"You bet I am," said Fox.

"Would you like to prove it?" said Mom.

"I'll get my bike," said Fox.

"Hold your horses," said Mom. "I have a better idea."

"Rats!" said Fox. "These aren't the wheels I had in mind!"

Think About It

1. In this story, how does Fox use wheels to play? *Well he race*
2. How does Fox use wheels to work?
3. Do you think Fox should have to mow the lawn? Why or why not?
4. Why is it dangerous to race shopping carts?

Create and Share

Pretend you are Fox's mother or father. Write what you would do if you wanted to teach Fox that racing shopping carts is wrong.

Explore

Find out about a race that really happened. Write down who won the race and what kind of race it was. Share what you learn with your class.

SONG of the TRAIN

Clickety-clack,
Wheels on the track,
This is the way
They begin the attack:
Click-ety-clack,
Click-ety-clack,
Click-ety-*clack*-ety,
Click-ety
Clack.

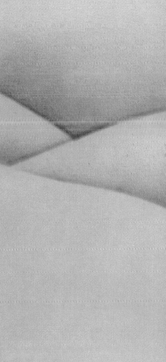

Clickety-clack
Over the crack,
Faster and faster
The song of the track:
Clickety-clack,
Clickety-clack,
Clickety, clackety,
Clackety
Clack.

Riding in front,
Riding in back,
Everyone hears
The song of the track:
Clickety-clack,
Clickety-clack,
Clickety, *clickety*,
Clackety
Clack.

—*David McCord*

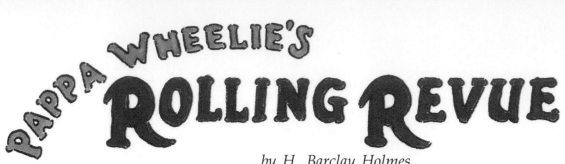

PAPPA WHEELIE'S ROLLING REVUE

by H. Barclay Holmes

Hello there, friends. Welcome to Pappa Wheelie's Rolling Revue. I'm Pappa Wheelie, your host. Today we are going to find out about the greatest invention of all time, the wheel.

All aboard! Back, back in time we go. The first stop will be 3800 B.C.

To our right is the ancient land of Mesopotamia. Historians think this is where the wheel began.

As far as the eye can see, slaves are dragging stone blocks to the city. It doesn't look too easy, does it?

Hey, look, someone put a round log under the rock. What a change! Now it's easier to move the rock.

But, *plop,* the log still gets stuck, and the rock tumbles off.

Historians think that after trying many other things, these smart people finally cut big wooden disks and put them on the ends of logs to make them roll over the bumps. At last, the wheel was born!

The wheel rolled right over the hilly ground, and the rocks didn't fall.

Look up ahead! We're coming to the green bumpy country of Scotland. The date is 1839. See that man in the workshop over there? That's Kirkpatrick Macmillan. He's working on his invention, the bicycle. I think he's almost finished.

I can hear a funny noise, can't you? Why, it's Kirkpatrick, riding the very first bicycle.

But look out, Kirkpatrick! *Crash— bump—bump.*

I guess our friend needs a little more practice.

Let's jump ahead 40 years, to Germany.

This time I smell something oily and smoky. I can hear something rumbling. Why, look! It's Karl Benz, on his three-wheeled car! It's the first gas-powered automobile!

Look, he's waving!

Karl, Karl, look out for that—*crash*—brick wall!

Oh, well, while Mr. Benz dusts himself off, let's return home to see what's new with the wheel.

Look! It's a country fair, and there are millions of wheels everywhere. Has the wheel changed that much? Not really. But look at all of its uses. Ferris wheels, merry-go-rounds. Carts and skateboards. Tractors and trucks and huge trains. How many things with wheels can you think of?

Think About It

1. Why is the poem "Song of the Train" called a song?
2. Name four ways you see the wheel being used in "Pappa Wheelie's Rolling Revue."
3. How do you think people traveled before the wheel was invented?
4. Why was the invention of the wheel so important?

Create and Share

Write about where you think the train in the poem is going, and why it is going there.

Explore

Find out what G.W.G. Ferris and Garrett Morgan invented.

Penelope Gets Wheels

by Esther Allen Peterson

It was Penelope's birthday, and she got
10 one dollar bills, 4 quarters, and 5 dimes.
She counted the money many times,
and it always came out the same: $11.50.

"I am rich and I am older now," she
said to her mom. "I don't need to walk
anymore. I will go on wheels."

"Wheels?" asked her mom.

"Yes," said Penelope. "I would like a car, but I know I am not rich enough or old enough. I think I will buy a bicycle."

"A bicycle costs a lot of money," said her mom.

"I have lots of money," Penelope said. Before her mother could say another word, Penelope ran outside and went to the store.

"Today is my birthday," she said to the salesperson. "I would like to buy that racing bike."

"That bicycle costs one hundred and nineteen dollars," the salesperson said.

Penelope pointed to a smaller bike. "How much is that one?"

"Seventy-nine dollars and ninety-five cents," said the salesperson.

"I'm not that rich," Penelope said, and she put the money back in her pocket.

Penelope looked at the badminton sets and baseball bats and gloves, but she didn't want to buy anything she saw.

Then she saw some roller skates. They were $9.95 a pair.

She picked up a skate and spun its wheels. "I guess these are all I can buy."

"That will be ten dollars and forty-five cents with tax," the salesperson said.

Penelope paid for the skates.

She went outside, put them on, and started skating home. She still wished she was old enough to drive a car or rich enough to own a bicycle.

When she got home her mom and dad were in the kitchen.

"I didn't have enough money for a bicycle," she said. "All I could buy were roller skates."

"Roller skates are the best wheels a kid can have," said her dad.

Penelope pushed one of the skates across the floor. "Skating is better than walking, but I'd still like to have a bike."

The next day everyone was going to the ball park to see Slugger Jones hit his five-hundredth home run. Slugger Jones was Penelope's favorite ballplayer, and she was going, too.

As she sat on the steps putting on her roller skates, Mr. Smith came out of his house and got into his car.

"Are you going to the game?" Penelope asked.

"I sure am," said Mr. Smith.

"I'm skating to the game," said Penelope.

"Be sure you don't get any speeding tickets," he said, and he drove off.

Penelope skated toward the ball park. Her friend Jim rode by on his bicycle.

"Going to the game?" she asked.

"Yep," he said.

"I am too," said Penelope.

"Let's race," said Jim.

Penelope skated as fast as she could, but Jim got ahead of her. Soon she couldn't see him at all.

Penelope skated fast for six blocks and then stopped. Cars were lined up waiting to get into the parking lot.

Penelope skated past Mr. Smith. "I didn't get any speeding tickets," she said.

"Really!" said Mr. Smith.

Near the ball park gate Penelope saw Jim looking for a place to lock his bike. She skated past him. "Does the winner get a prize?"

Penelope took off her skates, strapped them together, and waited in line to buy her ticket.

Then she went straight to her favorite seat.

Soon everyone stood up and sang the national anthem. The umpire yelled, *"Play ball!"*

Jim walked by looking for a seat.

During the second inning Mr. Smith came in.

Penelope giggled and said, "Roller skates are the best wheels a kid can have."

Think About It

1. At the end of the story, why does Penelope think roller skates are the best wheels a kid can have?

2. How does Penelope use wheels the same way Fox uses them?

3. How does Penelope use wheels in a different way?

4. Tell why you think people like riding on wheels so much.

Create and Share

Write about a trip you took on wheels. It could be real or make-believe. Your story could be called "(*Your Name*) on Wheels."

Explore

For one day, make a list of all the ways you see people using wheels to travel. Then share your list with your class.

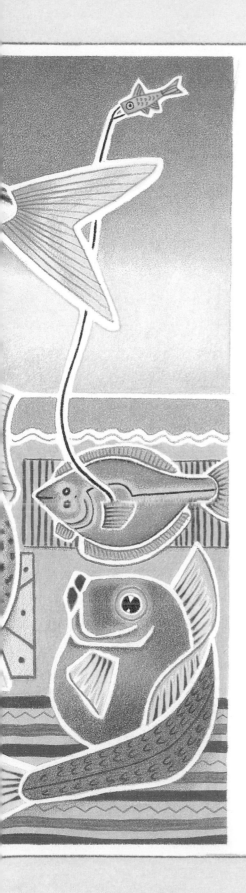

Sounds Fishy!

What fish loves mice? *(A catfish.)*

What is stranger than seeing
a catfish? *(Seeing a goldfish bowl.)*

Why can't you trust a shark?
(There's something fishy about it.)

The Fisherman and His Wife

retold by Anne L. Ryle

In a hut by the sea, a poor fisherman lived with his wife.

One day he pulled a big fish out of the shining blue sea. The fish said to him, "Please let me live. I am not a real fish. I am an enchanted prince."

"Oh," said the man. "I don't want a fish that can talk. Swim away!"

When the fisherman went home, he told his wife Ilsebil about the talking fish.

"Didn't you ask the fish for anything?" said his wife.

"No," said the man. "What should I ask for?"

"Ah," said Ilsebil. "I do not like this awful hut. Go back and tell the fish we want a pretty cottage instead of this awful hut."

The fisherman did not want to go, but he did. The sea looked all yellow and green. He called to the fish:

> Flounder, flounder in the sea,
> Come to me, O come to me!
> For my wife, good Ilsebil,
> Has a wish for you to fill.

"What do you want?" asked the fish.

"My wife does not like our hut. She wants a pretty cottage."

"Go home, then," said the fish. "You will find your wife in her cottage."

When the man got home, his wife said, "This cottage is much better than the hut."

"Ah!" said the fisherman. "How happy we'll be here."

"Maybe," said his wife.

Both of them were happy for a week. Then Ilsebil said, "This cottage is too small. Go and tell the fish to give us a castle."

The fisherman did not want to go, but he did. The sea looked all purple and gloomy. He called to the fish:

Flounder, flounder in the sea,
Come to me, O come to me!
For my wife, good Ilsebil,
Has a wish for you to fill.

"What do you want?" asked the fish.

"My wife wants to live in a castle," said the man sadly.

"Go home, then," said the fish. "She is there already."

When the man got home, his wife said, "Isn't this a grand castle?"

The fisherman said, "We'll be happy for the rest of our lives."

"Maybe," said Ilsebil.

The very next morning Ilsebil said, "I want to be king. Go and tell the fish I want to be king."

The fisherman did not want to go, but
he did. The sea was dark gray. He called
to the fish:

> *Flounder, flounder in the sea,*
> *Come to me, O come to me!*
> *For my wife, good Ilsebil,*
> *Has a wish for you to fill.*

"What do you want now?" asked the
fish.

"Alas," said the man, "my wife wants
to be king."

"Go home," said the fish. "She is king
already."

When the man got home, his wife said, "See! I am king!"

The fisherman looked at his wife's throne and her golden crown. "Now we have nothing more to wish for."

"I am tired of being king. Now I want to be emperor," said Ilsebil. "Go tell the fish I want to be emperor."

"Ah, Wife, I cannot ask for such a thing."

"I am king," said Ilsebil, "and you must do as I say. Go at once!"

The fisherman did not want to go, but he had to. "This is too much to ask and we will be sorry," he said to himself.

The sea was black and muddy. He called to the fish:

Flounder, flounder in the sea,
Come to me, O come to me!
For my wife, good Ilsebil,
Has a wish for you to fill.

"What do you want now?" asked the fish.

"I am sorry," said the fisherman, "but my wife wants to be emperor."

"Enough is enough!" said the fish. "You have asked for too much. Go home to your wife. She is in the hut again."

And there they live to this very day.

Think About It

1. Why doesn't the fish let Ilsebil be emperor?
2. Why does the ocean change color each time the fisherman goes back to see the fish?
3. How do you think the fisherman feels each time his wife asks for another wish?
4. What does this story say about asking for too much?

Create and Share

Pretend you are going to meet the characters in this story. Think about what you would like to ask them. Then write down your questions.

Explore

Read another fairy tale and think about the magic in the story.

Fish Do the Strangest Things

from the book by Leonora and Arthur Hornblow

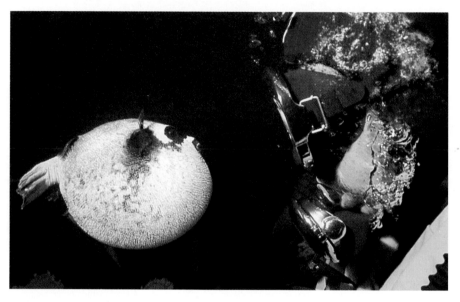

The Balloon

Fishermen catch many strange fish. One of the strangest fish of all is the puffer fish. The puffer fish is a small, slow swimmer. But it has a wonderful way of keeping itself safe. When it sees a big fish coming, it does not swim away. It just puffs itself up. It does this by swallowing air or water. This makes it look like a balloon.

The big fish may be scared away by this sudden change. If the big fish is not scared away, it will find that the round puffer is quite a mouthful.

The strangest puffer of all is called the porcupine fish. Its skin is covered with sharp spines. When it puffs itself up, its spines stick out all over. Any fish that swallowed it would have a very sore throat.

Sometimes puffers do a silly thing. They keep on puffing up and puffing up until—*pop* goes the puffer.

The Fish With Wings

The flying fish looks like a little airplane. But the flying fish does not fly. It glides.

The flying fish swims to the top of the water as fast as it can. It skims along for a bit. Then it flips its tail and up it goes.

We think the flying fish leaves the water to get away from its enemies. It can stay in the air for almost a minute. Then down it comes with a splash. Most times it will just flip its tail and take off again.

The winds may carry it high above the water. Sometimes at night flying fish will glide right onto the deck of a boat!

The Little Doctor

Most little fish get out of the way when they see a big fish coming. Most little fish are afraid the big fish will eat them. Most of the time the little fish are right.

There is one little fish that goes right up to the big fish. It puts its head in the big fish's mouth. It even swims between the teeth of the frightening moray eel. This strange little fish is called the wrasse.

Its name really should be the "little doctor fish." The little doctor cleans the teeth of the bigger fish. It cleans their eyes. It cleans their fins. It takes away little things which are growing on the other fish. These things would make the fish sick if the little doctor did not clean them off. That is why the wrasse is not hurt by the big fish. The big fish seem to know that the wrasse is helping them. They even wait their turn to see the wrasse. They are like people sitting in a real doctor's waiting room.

It is wonderful to think that fish have their own doctors, but this is only one of the wonders of the fish world.

People have always wanted to know more about the world of fish. It is a big world. There is more water in the world than there is land.

Maybe someday people will be able to live under water too. If this happens, who can tell what strange new things we will find out about our neighbors, the fish?

Think About It

1. How do the different fish you just read about stay safe?
2. Which fish do you think is the strangest?
3. If people did live under water someday, how do you think they would do it?

Create and Share

Draw a picture of one of the fish you read about. Write the name of the fish and what it is doing.

Explore

Read about another sea animal that does something strange.

THE FISH FROM JAPAN

by Elizabeth K. Cooper

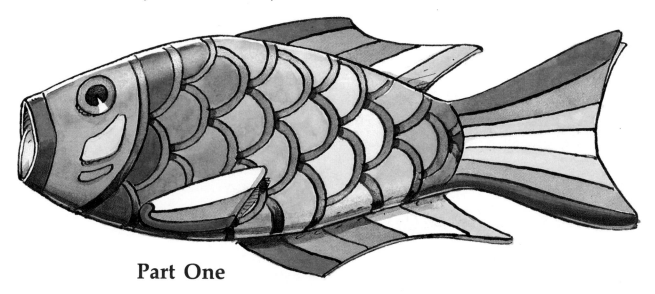

Part One

Harvey was early. He slipped into the room and looked around. No one, not even the teacher, was there. He ran to the cage and picked up the hamster.

"Hi, hamster," said Harvey.

The little brown hamster sat in Harvey's hand and blinked. Karla rushed in and saw Harvey with the hamster.

"Put that down!" she shouted. "That's my hamster!"

Harvey put the hamster back into its cage.

Karla began to feed her hamster.

"I wish I could help," said Harvey.

But Karla said, "No! Nobody else can feed my hamster. Go feed your own pets."

She went on feeding the hamster, and all Harvey could do was watch.

"I don't have a pet," Harvey said in a minute.

"Then get one," Karla said.

"I wish I could," said Harvey. "I'll ask my mother again, but I don't think it will do any good."

Harvey was right. When he asked his mother, she said the same old things. She had no time and no money for pets. She had all she could do just taking care of Harvey.

"But look," she said. "Here's a letter from Uncle Albert. He has a surprise for you."

There were six strange-looking stamps on the envelope.

"It came all the way across the ocean," said Harvey's mother. "Uncle Albert is going to send you a fish from Japan."

"A fish! When will I get it?" asked Harvey.

"Any day," said his mother.

Harvey could hardly wait to tell his friends.

The next morning in school he shared his news with his class.

"I am getting a pet!" he said. "My uncle is sending me a fish from Japan. When it comes, I will bring it to school to show."

The children were almost as eager as Harvey to see a fish from Japan, and so was the teacher.

At supper that night, Harvey's mother dished out some apple sauce. "I need that jar when it's empty," said Harvey.

"Here's one that's already empty," said his mother.

"That's not the right kind," said Harvey. "I want a jar I can see through, like glass."

"Oh, you mean transparent," said his mother. "I'll wash this one out, and then you can have it."

Harvey filled the transparent jar with water and carried it to his room. Then he sat in front of the jar and looked into the water. He was ready for his fish from Japan.

But the fish did not come the next day
nor the next.

Each morning in school the children
would ask, "Did you get your pet, Harvey?
Did you get the fish from Japan?"

All Harvey could say was, "No, not yet,
but the water is ready, and so is the jar. I
think the fish will be here tomorrow."

"He'll never get that fish!" said Karla.
"He just made it up."

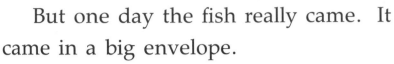

But one day the fish really came. It came in a big envelope.

"It must be a very flat fish," said Harvey to himself. "I hope it's not too big for my jar."

He ran to his room and opened the envelope.

There, at last, was the fish from Japan! It was made of colored paper and had a long string tied to its mouth. It was a kite.

Harvey looked at the kite. Then he put it back into the envelope, and hid it under some things in his closet.

Harvey sat down and looked and looked at the water in the transparent jar. If only the fish had been tiny and alive! Harvey could almost see it swimming around and around in the jar. Now what was he going to tell the other children in school?

Part Two

The next morning Harvey put a lid on the jar and took it to school early. He crept into the room and put the jar next to the hamster cage. As he was taking off the lid, Karla came in.

"What's that?" asked Karla.

"That's my fish from Japan," said Harvey. "It came yesterday."

Just then the bell rang, and the teacher came in with the other children.

"Harvey tells us that jar has his fish in it!" cried Karla. "But I can't see any fish."

"That's because it is transparent," said Harvey.

"What kind of fish?" asked the teacher.

"Transparent," said Harvey. "That means you can see right through it. It's hard to see a transparent fish in water."

Harvey took a small box from his pocket. "My fish eats transparent food," he said to the teacher. "I have to feed it three times a day, like this."

The teacher and all the children watched as Harvey fed his fish.

"Will you let me feed it sometime?" asked Karla.

"Maybe," said Harvey, "when you learn how."

At free time the children crowded around Harvey's jar. They all tried to see the transparent fish.

"There's nothing there but plain water," said a girl.

"But look, the water's moving!" said another girl. "That's where the fish is swimming and turning. It makes a tiny, tiny ripple."

"I almost saw it, too!" cried Karla.

Karla stared and stared at the water. Suddenly she shouted, "I think I saw one eye! It was round and shiny, and it looked right at me! You have to look hard to see it."

All the children looked harder than ever. They were very quiet until one boy began to jump up and down.

"I just saw the fins!" he said. "They're like little fans, and they go back and forth, like this." The boy used his hands to show how the fins moved in the water.

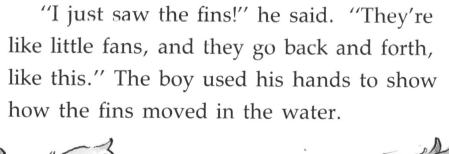

"Did you see the tail?" asked a girl. "There, in that sunny spot! It's long and wavy and has lots of colors. There! I just saw it again."

"So did I! So did I!" said the other children.

The children stared at the jar, and the teacher stared at the children.

"I never heard of this kind of fish before," she said.

Harvey looked up and smiled. "It's a very rare fish," he said. "It came all the way from Japan."

"Look at the mouth!" shouted a boy. "It opens and shuts, opens and shuts."

And the boy made a funny fish mouth with his lips. Another boy made a fish mouth with his hands.

"I think the fish is hungry," said Harvey. "Stand back. I'm going to feed it."

As he opened his little box of transparent food, he looked over at Karla. "You can feed it this time," said Harvey.

"Thanks, Harvey!" said Karla, and she fed the fish from Japan.

Harvey said that the fish needed rest after its lunch. The children tiptoed back to their seats, and the teacher put out the painting things.

The children began to paint. Everyone made a picture of Harvey's fish.

When the paintings were dry, the teacher put them up on the wall.

"Do you like them, Harvey?" she asked.

"What a fish!" said Harvey. "What a wonderful fish!"

When school was over, Harvey took his fish jar home with him.

The next morning Harvey came to school without the jar. The children ran to meet him.

"Where is your fish?" they asked.

"Gone!" said Harvey. "A cat sneaked into my room last night, and it ate the fish from Japan."

"That was awful," said Karla. And then she asked, "Do you want to help feed my hamster?"

"Sure!" said Harvey. "We can feed it together."

And that is what they did.

Think About It

1. At the beginning of the story, why doesn't Karla let Harvey feed her hamster?
2. Why does she change her mind at the end of the story?
3. If you were Harvey, what would you have done if your pet fish had turned out to be a kite?
4. Think about the fish you have read about in SOUNDS FISHY! How is each fish strange?

Create and Share

Draw a picture of a make-believe fish. Write a sentence about your fish under your picture.

Explore

Read about how to take care of pet fish.

Pick a Pet

Beagle 8 wks. old,
good with kids, free
to good home, 555-8974

ELEPHANT for SALE

Elephant for sale!
Elephant for sale!
One big, beautiful
Elephant for sale!

He'll tell you a story
When you go to bed.
He'll fluff your pillow
And pat your head.

Elephant for sale!
Elephant for sale!
One big, beautiful
Elephant for sale!

He'll wash the dishes.
He'll mop the floor.
He'll carry out the trash
And do lots more.

Elephant for sale!
Elephant for sale!
One big, beautiful
Elephant for sale!

He'll tell you a joke.
He'll sing you a song.
He'll tell you a story
That's not too long.

Elephant for sale!
Elephant for sale!
Onc big, beautiful
Elephant for sale!

Mom says to sell him.
She says "Sell him right now."
She doesn't believe
He's an overgrown cow.

Elephant for sale!
Elephant for sale!
One big, beautiful
Elephant for sale!

I want to keep him
But Mom says "No!"
And that's the reason
He has to go.

Elephant for sale!
Elephant for sale!
One big, beautiful
Elephant for sale!

—*Maurice Poe*

Alison Chooses a Pet

by Stephen Krensky

Alison was excited. She was going to the pet store. She had never been to a pet store before. Today she was going to get her first pet.

Alison wanted to pick out her pet very carefully. But how would she start? There must be many animals in a pet store.

"I want it to be special," she thought.

A lion would be special. The lion is the king of beasts. Alison could make the lion a crown. He and she could be king and queen of the backyard jungle.

"Uh, oh," thought Alison.

She remembered that lions like to roar.
What if the lion roared at her in the middle
of the night?

Maybe a dolphin would be better. A
dolphin wouldn't roar. A dolphin would
be quiet. She could build a big pool for it.
They would take long swims and tell each
other secrets.

"Uh, oh," thought Alison.

What if the pool leaked into the living room? The dolphin might end up sitting on the couch. Everything would be very wet.

Maybe a bear would be better. A bear didn't need a pool. A bear could walk beside her. They could eat honey together and climb trees all afternoon.

"Uh, oh," thought Alison.

Bears also sleep for the whole winter.
What if the bear fell asleep in her bed? She
might tug and tug at the bear and never
move it. She would have no place to sleep
herself.

Maybe a rhinoceros would be better. A
rhino wouldn't sleep so much. She could
ride it to school. They could play hide-and-
seek at recess.

"Uh, oh," thought Alison.

What if the rhino wasn't careful with its horn? It might poke holes in her pillows when they played hide-and-seek at home. Feathers would fly everywhere.

Maybe a gorilla would be better. A gorilla has no horns. It has long arms. A gorilla could swing both ends of a jump rope while Alison jumped in the middle.

"Uh, oh," thought Alison.

Sometimes the gorilla might use its arms
for other things. What if it swung from the
light in the living room and carried her
father around on its back?

Maybe a giraffe would be better. A
giraffe couldn't swing from anything.
A giraffe had no arms. But a giraffe had
a long neck. Alison could slide down its
neck from a tree.

"Uh, oh," thought Alison.

A giraffe wouldn't fit in the house. Her parents would have to cut holes in the roof.

Maybe a crocodile would be better. A crocodile is short. She could make it a leash and go for walks with it in the park.

"Uh, oh," thought Alison.

What if the crocodile saw some ducks? It might break its leash and waddle after them.

"Come back here, Crocodile!" she cried, running down the street.

Alison stopped. She had reached the pet store. She was out of breath. The lion and dolphin and bear and rhinoceros and gorilla and giraffe and crocodile had worn her out.

Alison looked in the store window. A hamster was sitting on a wheel. Alison looked at the hamster. She thought the hamster looked back.

Alison marched into the store. She asked for the hamster in the window.

"How did you choose a pet so fast?" asked the owner.

"It was easy," said Alison. "A hamster doesn't roar. It doesn't need a big pool. It won't sleep all winter. It has no horns. It can't swing from the lights. It's very short and it won't eat ducks."

"So what will the hamster do?" the owner asked.

Alison smiled. "The hamster will be my friend," she said.

She paid for the hamster and took it home. They were good friends for a long time.

Think About It

1. Why do you think the elephant is for sale in the poem "Elephant for Sale"?
2. How are the elephant and the pets Alison thinks about the same?
3. Could Alison have found any of the pets she thought about at the pet store? Why or why not?
4. Why is a hamster a good pet for Alison?

Create and Share

If you could choose one animal in this story to have as a pet, which would you choose? Write about what you would do with this animal.

Explore

Read about the animal you chose as a pet. Find out what kinds of habits that animal has.

A First Pet for You

from YOUR FIRST PET AND HOW TO TAKE CARE OF IT
by *Carla Stevens*

You want a pet that you can take care of yourself, but what kind of pet? Before you make up your mind, think about what it will mean to you to own a living animal.

Remember that a pet cannot live without you. It cannot catch its own food to eat or find its own water to drink. It cannot clean its own cage. A pet is not a toy. When you get tired of a toy, you put it away and forget about it. You cannot ever forget your pet. Your pet will need you, or someone like you, to take care of it all of its life.

If you are sure that you can take good care of an animal, then it is time to choose your pet. Two kinds of animals that make good pets are hamsters and kittens.

A Golden Hamster

The hamster is a kind of animal that lives well in a cage. The golden hamster looks like a tiny, furry teddy bear. It has a very short tail. It has large cheek pouches where it stores food or litter. A hamster's front teeth are very sharp.

To make a home for a hamster, you will need a hamster cage. The hamster cage should have a pan that can be removed and cleaned. Put some papers on the bottom of the pan. Then fill the pan with at least 2 inches of hay or hamster litter for bedding. The papers will help to keep the bedding in the cage.

Don't leave the cage in direct sunlight. Hamsters do not need a lot of sunshine.

Now you can put your hamster in its cage. Don't try to take the hamster out for a few days. Let it get used to its new home.

To feed your hamster, you can buy hamster food. Hamsters will also eat carrots, lettuce, apples, and nuts. Put fresh food out for your hamster every day but don't give it too much.

If you give your hamster more food than it can eat at one time, it will put the food in its cheek pouches. You will know when the hamster is hiding its food. Its cheeks will be very puffed out.

Clean the hamster's cage once a week. First put your hamster in a safe place. A large box will do. Take out the bottom pan and dump the newspaper and bedding into a large bag to be thrown away. Wash the pan with soap and water. Scrub the corners with a brush. Rinse the pan with plain water. Dry it and slide it back into the cage. Put clean papers and bedding in the pan.

When your hamster is used to its new home, you can begin to tame it. This will take some time. You must pick your hamster up every day. If your pet seems easily frightened, it is a good idea to use gloves. The hamster might bite.

Put your hand slowly in the cage. Let the hamster sniff your hand. Then lift the hamster slowly and hold it firmly so that it will not be afraid of falling. Each time you pick your hamster up, give it something good to eat. Soon your hamster will grow used to you.

A Kitten

A kitten is a good pet, too. It will have fun climbing onto high shelves and playing with you!

When your kitten comes to live with you, it should be 8 weeks old, or even older. That way your new kitten will get used to its new home more easily.

There are two things you must have for your kitten when it arrives. Your kitten needs a place to sleep and a litter pan. The place to sleep can be a box or a basket with a soft blanket.

Help your pet to know that this is its special place. Put your kitten in its box or basket when it is sleepy. Then stroke your kitten gently until it purrs.

You can buy litter and a litter pan from your pet store. It is sold in 10- and 25-pound bags. Fill the pan with at least 4 inches of litter. Put the pan inside a large box. Leave the top of the box and one side open.

It takes only a day or two for your kitten to learn to use the pan.

Clean the litter box each day. Change the litter about once a week.

Your kitten should be fed three times a day, from 8 weeks on. After your kitten is 6 months old, it only needs two meals a day.

A cat must have something to scratch. If your kitten does not scratch, its claws will grow so long that it will have trouble walking. Give your cat something of its own to scratch. Then your pet won't claw your rugs or chairs.

Pet stores sell scratching posts. If your pet still scratches your things, rub some catnip on the scratching post. Most cats love catnip!

Kittens love to play. Playing is good for your kitten too. With a piece of string, a ball, or a paper bag, your kitten and you can have lots of fun.

Hamsters and kittens are just two animals that make good pets. By reading about other animals and going to a pet store, you can find just the right pet for you.

Think About It

1. What do you have to think about before you decide to get a pet?
2. Why do hamsters and kittens make good pets?
3. In the last story, Alison gets a hamster for a pet. What will she have to do to take care of it?
4. What are some other animals that make good pets?

Create and Share

Write about how to keep another kind of pet happy, clean, and fed.

Explore

Ask ten people what kind of pet they have. Make a chart with your answers and share it with your class. Be sure to include the number of people that have no pets.

The Crab

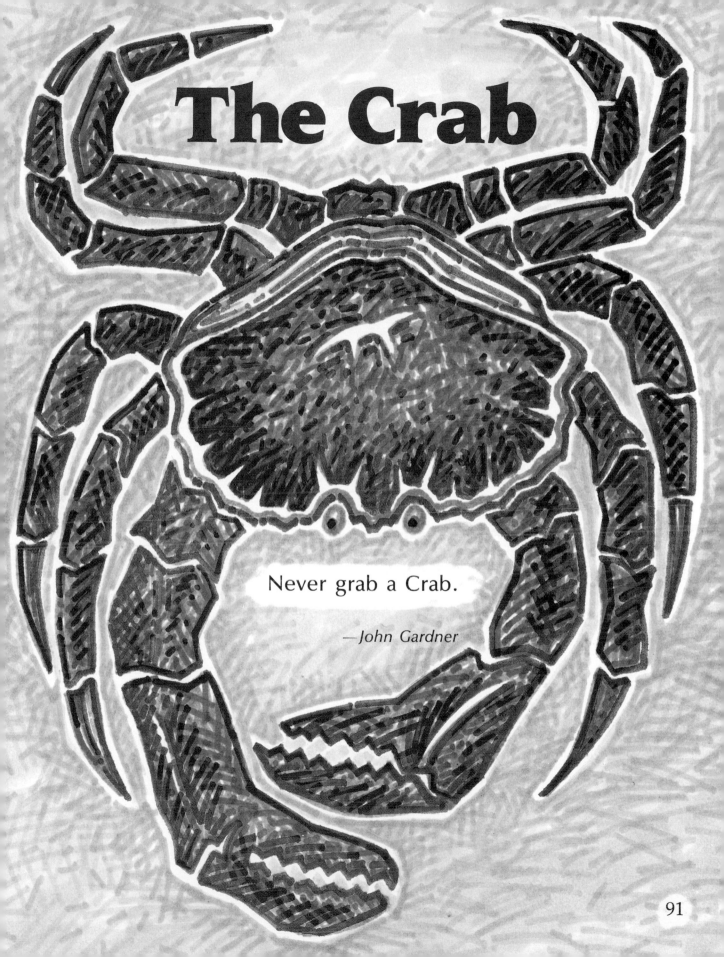

Never grab a Crab.

—*John Gardner*

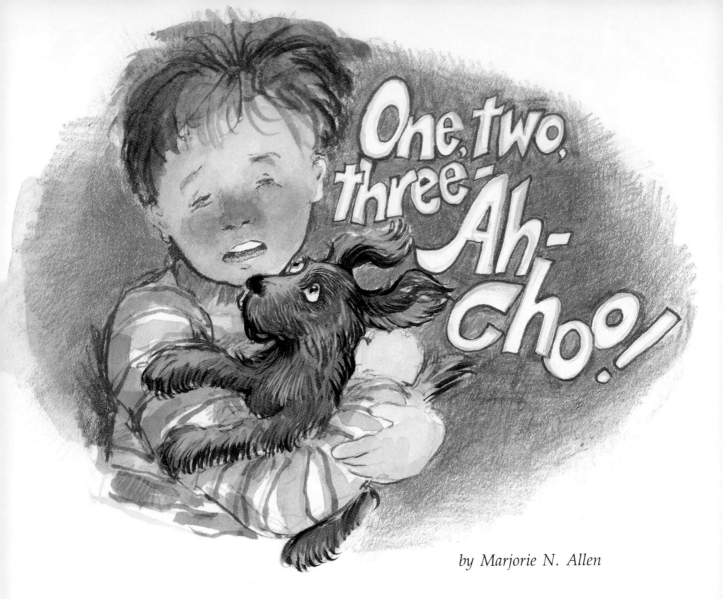

by Marjorie N. Allen

Fur and Feathers

Wally Springer had a problem. He had many allergies. Dust made him sneeze. Feathers made him sneeze. Now he had just found out his puppy made him sneeze.

"The doctor says you are allergic to animal fur," said his mother. "And I'm afraid your allergy shots won't help."

92

"Why me?" he groaned. "Other people can have dogs or cats. But not me. I'm allergic to pets." He took his medicine and made a face.

"Not all pets have fur and feathers," said his mother. "We'll just have to find one that won't make you sneeze."

No More Sneezes

Wally stared at the fishbowl. Inside, four tadpoles wiggled and swam. They swam around and around. "Tadpoles," said Wally, "are boring."

"Just wait," said his mother. Wally waited and waited. At least tadpoles didn't make him sneeze.

After a few weeks the tadpoles began to sprout legs.

Their tails became shorter and shorter. They changed color. After a few more weeks, they stopped swimming and sat on a large rock in the fishbowl.

Now they were frogs. Singing frogs. Jumping frogs. "I can't stand it," said Wally's father. "They sing all night long. They sound like fingernails scratching a blackboard."

Wally didn't like the noise either. The frogs had kept him awake the whole night.

Sausages

"Frogs are all right," said Wally. "But snakes are better."

He found a home for his frogs in a pond. There he picked up a beautiful Banded Water Snake. She was creamy white with dark bands. She wrapped herself around Wally's arm. Wally called her Sheila. "Snakes don't eat in winter," he told his parents. "They sleep all winter."

When winter came, Wally took Sheila out of her terrarium and put her in a cloth bag. He put the bag in the refrigerator.

"A snake in my refrigerator!" his mother cried.

"It's all right," said Wally. "She's way in the back. You'll forget she's there. She'll sleep all winter." Wally was right.

Everyone forgot about Sheila—until December. In December, Aunt Betty came to visit. Aunt Betty made herself right at home. "Ah—sausage!" she said. She pulled the cloth bag from the refrigerator and set it on a dish. "I'll have a snack before dinner," Aunt Betty said. Soon Sheila warmed up.

Just as Aunt Betty picked up the bag to take out the sausage, the snake began to move. Aunt Betty screamed. Mother dropped a dish. Father dropped a cup of milk. Aunt Betty dropped Sheila.

"No snakes in the refrigerator," said Wally's mother.

Seashells

Wally put Sheila back in her terrarium. Now he had to feed her. He called the pet store. "What do snakes eat in winter?" he asked.

"Live mice," the store clerk said.

Wally shuddered. He could never feed a live mouse to a snake. Besides, mice made him sneeze. Wally didn't know what to do.

"I have an idea," said the pet store clerk. "Send me your snake. I will send you a new pet."

"I'm allergic to fur and feathers," said Wally.

"This pet doesn't have fur or feathers," said the store clerk.

"Does it sing at night? Does it eat live mice?" asked Wally.

"No, none of those things," said the clerk. Wally could not think of what the store clerk would send. He put Sheila in a box, and his father took her to the pet store. Wally couldn't go. Pet stores made him sneeze.

He sat by the window, waiting for his father to come back. When he saw the car, he ran to the door. "Here is your new pet," his father said.

He handed Wally a seashell. It was white with brown stripes. "A seashell?" Wally asked.

"More than a seashell," said his father. "Put it on the table."

The seashell skittered across the table.
"It's alive!" Wally yelled.

"It's a hermit crab," said his father.
"Here is a book all about them." Wally
picked up the seashell and put it in the
terrarium. Then he sat down to read
the book.

> *Hermit crabs make fun pets.*
> *As the crab grows, it changes its shell*
> *for a new one. It makes its home in*
> *the cast-off shells of other sea animals.*

Wally knew he would have to get some
larger shells. He called his hermit crab
Harold. He fed him cake crumbs.

"Junk food!" said his mother.

"He also likes lettuce," said Wally. "Besides, he only eats once every two months."

"Well . . . all right," she said.

The book was right. Hermit crabs were fun. And best of all, they didn't make Wally sneeze. But when Harold won a prize at the neighborhood pet show in the park, Wally had to walk past the dogs and cats and hamsters to pick up his prize.

The judges said, "Congratulations!"

"Ah-choo! Ah-choo! Ah-choo!" said Wally.

Think About It

1. Why is a hermit crab a good pet for Wally?
2. After reading the poem "The Crab," what do you think Wally should be careful of?
3. How were Wally's and Alison's problems the same?
4. How were their problems different?
5. Of all the pets you read about in PICK A PET, which pet would you like to have? Tell why.

Create and Share

Write a rhyming poem like "The Crab." Fill in the blanks. Never ____ a ____.

Explore

Read another poem about a pet. Look up the poets Aileen Fisher and Shel Silverstein for ideas.

Music-makers

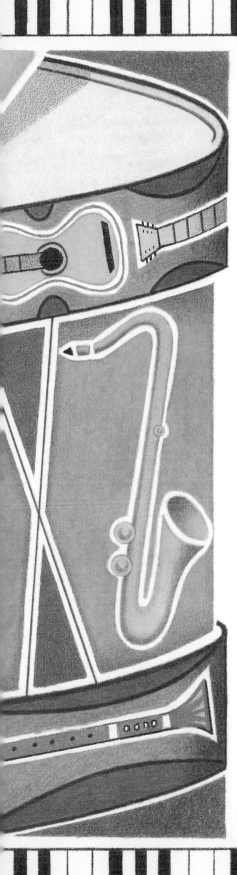

A tooter who tooted a flute
Tried to tutor two tooters to toot.
Said the two to the tutor,
"Is it harder to toot, or
To tutor two tooters to toot?"

Jasper Makes Music

by Betty Horvath

Jasper wanted a guitar that he could carry around and strum to make music. He had wanted it for a long time. Then he saw the guitar in the window of a music store. He knew that it was the *very* guitar he wanted. He had to have it.

Jasper saw the price tag on the guitar. He didn't have any money.

He turned his pockets inside out. One pocket held a gum wrapper and a piece of string. The other had nothing in it. Jasper had no money at all. He pressed his face up to the window until his nose was squashed flat, and he looked and looked.

All the way home he thought about the guitar. He hummed a little.

"If I had that old guitar," he told himself, "I could sit out on the front-porch steps and sing."

He ran to find his mother. "There's something I need," Jasper told her.

His mother looked at Jasper's feet. "I'll bet I can guess," she said. "You need a new pair of shoes."

"No," said Jasper, "that's not it. I need a guitar."

His mother laughed. "No, Jasper. You just *want* a guitar. What you *need* is shoes."

Jasper turned away sadly. He didn't need shoes. He didn't even want shoes. What he needed and wanted was a real guitar of his own.

"Maybe I can make a guitar," Jasper thought.

He found an empty box. His big brother Paul helped him nail a thin piece of wood to it for a neck. Then they strung it with rubber bands.

Jasper took his guitar out on the front-porch steps. He started to sing and play. But no matter how hard he tried, his guitar just didn't sound like a guitar at all. It sounded like an old box strung with rubber bands. Jasper put it down.

A week went by. Jasper got a new pair of shoes.

A month went by. He got a winter coat because it was getting colder now. Winter was coming.

One Saturday morning when Jasper woke up, he heard Grandpa's voice coming from the kitchen. "Get up, Jasper! We've got work to do today."

Jasper dressed quickly. Working with Grandpa was a treat. "What are we going to do today, Grandpa?" he asked.

Grandpa pointed out the window. "See those squirrels? They know winter is coming. They're busy storing up food for the winter, and that's what we're going to do, too. We're going to be squirrels."

Jasper thought about being a squirrel. He thought about Grandpa being a squirrel. He almost laughed out loud.

Then he saw that the kitchen floor was covered with jar after jar of corn, peas, and beans that his mother had been canning all summer long.

"I know!" he said, pointing. "These are our acorns and we're going to store them in the cellar."

"Right!" said Grandpa. "But before we store our food away we've got a job to do. We have to clean the cellar out first."

Grandpa handed Jasper a broom. He and Jasper went down the back steps into the room under the house.

They began to work. It was hard work sweeping the floor and dusting off all the shelves, but it was kind of like a treasure hunt, too. Jasper kept finding things he hadn't seen for a long time. He found his baseball that had been missing most of the summer. He found an old roller skate and a ball. Then Jasper saw the handle of something half hidden behind some boxes. He pulled it out. It was a small shovel.

"Look what I found, Grandpa!" he shouted.

Grandpa picked it up. "Why, I believe you've found the magic shovel I gave your daddy when he was about your size."

"A magic shovel! What's magic about it?" Jasper asked.

"It's magic because you can get things you wish for with it. If I remember right, it got your daddy a bike."

"Oh, boy!" said Jasper, thinking about the guitar. "How does it work?"

"Well, that's the funny thing," Grandpa said. "Part of the magic has to do with the person who owns it. Part of the magic has to do with the weather, too, because it's a snow shovel. You'd be surprised how much money a boy can earn shoveling snow with a magic shovel." Grandpa smiled and winked at Jasper.

Jasper winked back.

They moved all the jars into the cellar. Then Jasper cleaned his magic shovel until it shone. He stood it on the back porch to wait for the first snowy day.

Up and down the street he went. He knocked on doors and asked his neighbors if he could be their winter snow-shoveler.

"I've got a magic shovel," he told them, "and if I wish hard enough and work hard enough I'll earn enough money to buy a guitar."

Mrs. Adams said No, she didn't need a snow-shoveler.

But Mrs. James and Miss Daniels and Mr. Arthur said Yes, Jasper could shovel their snow all winter long for fifty cents every time it snowed.

Then Jasper did one more thing. He needed a bank to keep his money in. He took an empty can, covered it with white paper, and printed on it, **guitar money**.

He was all ready for the first snowfall.

Then one day the snow began to fall. It
fell and fell and fell.

Jasper shoveled and shoveled and
shoveled. He whistled while he worked.
He knew that by the time it was warm
enough again to sit out on the front-porch
steps and sing, he'd have a real guitar of
his own to strum.

Think About It

1. What does Jasper do to show you that he really wants a guitar?
2. Do you think Jasper earned enough money to buy the guitar? Write what you think happened when springtime came.
3. Have you ever saved your money to buy something? Tell about it.
4. Why do you think people like making music?

Create and Share

If you could buy an instrument, what kind would you buy? Write why you would make that choice.

Explore

Find out what kind of music one of these famous music makers made—J.S. Bach, Louis Armstrong, Joan Baez.

Make Your Own Instruments

by Judy Hall

It's fun and easy to make musical instruments from things you find around the house. You can turn a comb into a harmonica, or a cooking pot into a drum! Follow the directions below and in no time you'll be playing in your own band!

Box Strings

Take the lid off of a small box. Find four rubber bands of different sizes. Stretch them around the box, starting with the smallest rubber band and ending with the largest.

To play your box strings, pluck or strum the rubber bands.

Comb Harmonica

Fold a small piece of tracing paper in half and place over the teeth of a small comb. Hold the comb and paper against your lips and hum a tune.

Water Glass Vibes

Line up four or more water glasses and put some water in the first glass. Put a little more water in each of the other glasses as shown.

To play, tap the water glasses with a spoon.

Kitchen Percussion

Look around your kitchen for things you can use as drums and drumsticks. Here are some things you can use. Can you think of more?

Drums	Drumsticks
Trash Can	New Pencils
Cooking Pot	Chopsticks
Empty Cans	Spoons
Lids	

Now, get together with your friends and start your own band!

Think About It

1. What kind of music do you think these instruments make?
2. Which kind of instrument is like the one that Jasper tried to make?
3. Where would you find the things needed for making these instruments?
4. Do you know of other ways to make musical instruments? Explain how.

Create and Share

Make one of the instruments you just read about. Use the instrument in the play that you will read next.

Explore

Count how many times in a day you hear music. Don't forget music on TV or in music class. What kind of music do you like best?

THE BREMEN-TOWN MUSICIANS

retold by H. Barclay Holmes

Characters

Mr. Burro, the farm donkey

Miss Growlin, an old hunting dog

Whiskers, a tired cat

Chanticleer, a soon-to-be-soup rooster

Robber 1, a bad guy

Robber 2, a worse guy

Scene One

(*Old* Mr. Burro *is walking down a dirt path.*)

Mr. Burro: Well, I'm too old
To carry loads,
Or pull a cart
Down dusty roads!

So, bye old farm!
I'm off today
To Bremen-town
To sing and play.

Scene Two

(Mr. Burro *sees an old dog in the road.*)

Miss Growlin: Oh, please, please, please!
Don't step on me!
I'm just too old,
I'm fifty-three!

I cannot hunt.
I cannot run.
My master says
That I'm no fun!

Mr. Burro: Why, you're not old!
I think you're wrong!
Why, come with me
And sing a song!

Miss Growlin: Oh, can I really?
Oh, can I come?
I'll sing and dance!
And beat the drum!

Mr. Burro: Why sure! Let's go!
To play and sing
In Bremen-town,
A ring-a-ding-ding!

Scene Three

(The two new friends see a very sad old cat.)

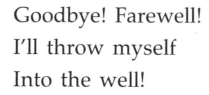

Whiskers: Meow, meow!
Goodbye! Farewell!
I'll throw myself
Into the well!

Oh, I'm too old
To catch a mouse.
Why, I'm not welcome
In my own house!

So, what will I do?
Where will I go?

Mr. Burro: Why, come with us!
Come, join our show!

Whiskers: Why sure! Let's go!
To play and sing
In Bremen-town.
A ring-a-ding-ding!

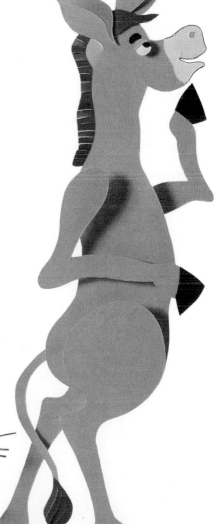

Scene Four

(*The three musicians hear a loud voice.*)

Miss Growlin: Why, what's that sound?

Whiskers: It's Chanticleer.
He tells the time
Throughout the year!

(Mr. Burro *calls up to* Chanticleer.)

Mr. Burro: You sound as if
You are in danger!
What can it be?
Please tell us, stranger!

Chanticleer: Why, I'm in trouble!
I've gotta whoop!
Or I will soon be
rooster soup!

Miss Growlin: So, why not leave?
Come, join our band!
For when you sing,
It is so grand!

Chanticleer: Why, sure! Let's go!
To play and sing
In Bremen-town,
A ring-a-ding-ding!

(*The four walk on into the night.*)

Whiskers: Oh, look there, friends!
I see a light!
It's just the place
To spend the night!

Scene Five

(*They come to the house and look in the window.*)

Mr. Burro: I can't believe it!
It's not true!
There's Robber 1
And Robber 2!

Chanticleer: Why, we'll never eat!
We'll waste away!
We'll never sing
Another day!

Mr. Burro: Don't you worry,
Don't you fret!
Don't give up,
No, no, not yet!

We'll make a plan,
We'll scare those men.
We'll sing our song,
Then sing it again!

So, when I count,
Sing loud and clear.
Let's let them know
That we are here!

One, two, three . . .

All: And fiddly-dee!
Yadda-yadda boom-boom!
Big honey bee!

Zim, zam zoomy!
Beetly boy!
Rim, ram roomy!
Hobbledehoy!

(*The robbers run out yelling.*)

Robber 1: Goblins, ghoulies,
Terrible snakes!

Robber 2: We've been attacked,
For goodness' sake!

Whiskers: Hooray, we've done it!
They've gone away!
Let's eat and sing
And dance and play!

(*They eat their fill and fall asleep.*)

(*The* Robbers *are angry!*)

Robber 1: There are no ghouls
Or monsters there!
Just howling winds
And whistling air!

(Robber 1 *points to* Robber 2.)

Robber 1: So you go back,
Without a fear,
To check and see
If the coast is clear!

(*The scared robber goes back in and steps on sleeping Whiskers's tail.*)

Whiskers: Meow, meeoow!

Miss Growlin: A ruff, a rooo!

Mr. Burro: Hee-haw, hee-haw!

Chanticleer: Cock-a-doodle-do!

(*The robbers scream and run far from the house.*)

Miss Growlin: Hooray! We've done it!

They're really gone!

Now we can dance

And sing our song!

Whiskers: Oh boy! Let's go!

Let's play and sing

In Bremen-town,

A ring-a-ding-ding!

(Chanticleer *looks troubled*.)

Chanticleer: But, wait a minute!

Let's not hurry!

This trip to Bremen

Makes me worry . . .

Well . . . Why go off

To Bremen-town?

We'll scare the folks!

We'll make them frown!

Mr. Burro: Why, you're so right,
Dear Chanticleer!
We've all we need.
Let's stay right here!

Miss Growlin: Why sure! Let's stay!
Let's play and sing!
We're home at last!
A ring-a-ding-ding!

All: One, two, three . . .
And fiddly-dee!
Yadda-yadda boom-boom
Big honey bee!

Zim, zam zoomy!
Beetly boy!
Rim, ram roomy!
Hobbledehoy!

(So they lived and sang forevermore.)

Balancing Act

A sea horse saw a sawhorse
On a seesaw meant for two.
"See here, sawhorse," said sea horse,
"May I seesaw with you?"

"I'll see, sea horse," said sawhorse.
"Right now I'm having fun
Seeing if I'll be seasick
On a seesaw meant for one."

SEA HORSE AND SAWHORSE
by X. J. Kennedy

The Balancing Girl

by Berniece Rabe

Margaret was very good at balancing. She could balance a book on her head. She could glide along in her wheelchair and the book would not fall off.

She could even balance herself and hop with her crutches.

At school she collected the Magic Markers. She would balance them in neat rows on the shelf. The teacher said, "You have a very steady hand, Margaret."

Tommy said, "Anybody can do that. Who couldn't do that?"

Right while Tommy watched, Margaret balanced twenty blocks in a tower.

"That's simple," he said.

"Then you do it," said Margaret.

But Tommy wouldn't try. He just said, "I still say it's simple."

Margaret planned and planned. She wanted to do something very special that Tommy could not call simple.

She got out of her wheelchair. She pushed some regular chairs together just so, and she made a special corner for her work.

It took a long time, but at last she was done. She had made a tall castle out of blocks and cans.

The other kids clapped for the castle.

Tommy said, "That's simple. I build castles like that all the time."

Margaret would have yelled at him if the teacher had not said, "Time for recess."

After recess, Margaret's castle was knocked down.

Margaret looked at Tommy.

Tommy yelled, "I don't know who did it!"

Margaret still stared at him. She said, "Tommy, you had better never knock down anything I balance again. If you do, *you'll be sorry!*"

Tommy was just starting to yell back when the teacher came back. Margaret hoped that the teacher would yell at Tommy, but he didn't.

The teacher said, "We are going to hold a school carnival. We need ideas for carnival booths."

Quickly Tommy raised his hand. "My big brother had a carnival at his school. He and my dad ran a fishpond. People paid to fish for presents. My dad and I could run a fishpond booth."

Everyone clapped for Tommy's idea. Even Margaret clapped.

"Good," said the teacher. "Are there any other ideas?"

William said, "I want to be a clown."

Tommy laughed. "Clowns don't make money."

Margaret raised her hand. She said, "I saw a clown once who sold balloons." Margaret liked William.

"That's the kind of clown I will be," said William. "I will be a balloon-selling clown."

None of the other children raised their hands.

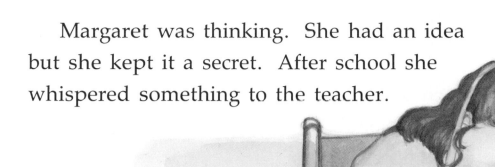

Margaret was thinking. She had an idea but she kept it a secret. After school she whispered something to the teacher.

The next day Margaret took some dominoes to a corner of the room. In the corner she started setting up the dominoes. Very gently, very carefully she placed each domino. Each was just a little way away from the one before it. She had to be very, very careful. If one fell, it would knock the next one down. Then one by one they would all come toppling down.

Everyone watched Margaret. They asked her what she was doing.

She told them it was her secret. Margaret made fancy curves and snaky S's. She used up all the dominoes in the classroom. The teacher gave her more dominoes to use.

She made little stairs with the dominoes. She made little roads and highways with the dominoes. It looked like a little city.

The teacher said it was time for recess.

Tommy grabbed the great big ball. He gave it two big bounces. It would have bounced right into Margaret's corner. But William jumped and caught it. Margaret was glad her dominoes didn't get knocked down.

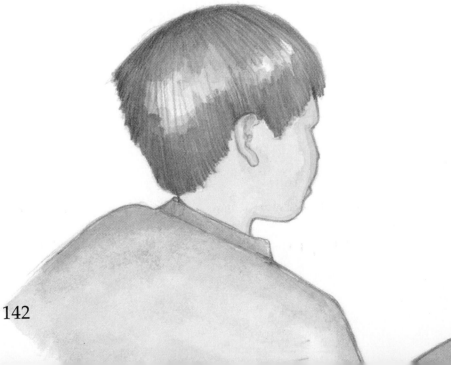

The next day Margaret finished placing
the last domino. Everyone begged to be
the one to push down the first domino.
Even Tommy begged to be the one.

Margaret said, "The name of the one to
do that will be pulled out of a hat. You
will have to pay to get your name in that
hat."

The teacher said, "The name will be
drawn from the hat the night of the
school carnival."

Everyone clapped. Margaret was very
happy and pleased.

WHITMAN SCHOOL CARNIVAL

FISH FOR PRIZE

FIS
FO
PRI

144

Finally, it was the day of the carnival.

Margaret visited every booth. William sold her three balloons. She tied the balloons to her wheelchair.

Then she went to visit Tommy's booth. Tommy was standing out in the hall. He was watching people go up to his booth.

Margaret asked, "Why aren't you working, Tommy?"

Tommy answered, "My Dad has too much help. I guess he's got a hundred people helping him. Even my big brother is helping."

"Oh," said Margaret. She fished in the pond booth anyway. She got a rubber spider.

At last it was time to push down the first domino at Margaret's booth.

Everyone moved along to the second grade room.

Margaret waited until everyone was in the room. She began to draw the name from the hat. Everyone looked at each other and then at Margaret.

Margaret looked at the paper and read, "Tommy Perkins."

Tommy went to the front of the crowd. He stepped inside the domino corner. He stood there for a long time, looking at Margaret.

"Well, push," said Margaret.

Tommy pushed harder than was needed, but still it went beautifully. *Click, click, click,* a thousand times *click*, the dominoes took their turns falling. It seemed like it took hours for them all to fall.

A big cheer went up!

Then Tommy looked right at Margaret.

He yelled, "There! I knocked down something that you balanced, and I'm not sorry."

"I'm not sorry either," called back Margaret. "My booth made the most money in this carnival."

"Hurray for the Balancing Girl," someone shouted.

And Margaret was sure she heard Tommy join in with the big cheer that went up.

Think About It

1. Why is "The Balancing Girl" a good name for Margaret?
2. Why do you think Tommy tries to knock down what Margaret balances?
3. Why is it important for Margaret to balance something that Tommy will not call simple?
4. Do you think Tommy likes Margaret's domino booth? Tell why or why not.

Create and Share

Think of different ways people use balance. Make a list of your ideas.

Explore

Find out how Peggy Fleming used balance to become famous.

Making a Mobile

by Ellen Hopkins

Giant lollipops twirl around in the wind. A fish floats in the air. How is this possible? Alexander Calder, a famous sculptor, made it possible by inventing the mobile. The word *mobile* means "able to move." In art, a mobile is a balancing piece of sculpture. Objects hang from thin wire. When the wind blows, the objects move through the air.

Calder wanted his art to move the way things in real life move. At first he used motors to make his sculpture move. But the objects could move only in one direction and often the motors broke down. Then he thought of hanging his sculpture in the air so that it could move freely.

Today Calder's mobiles hang in museums, banks, airports, and parks. People all over the world enjoy his work.

Simple mobiles are easy and fun to make. The directions on the next few pages will show you how you can make your own mobile.

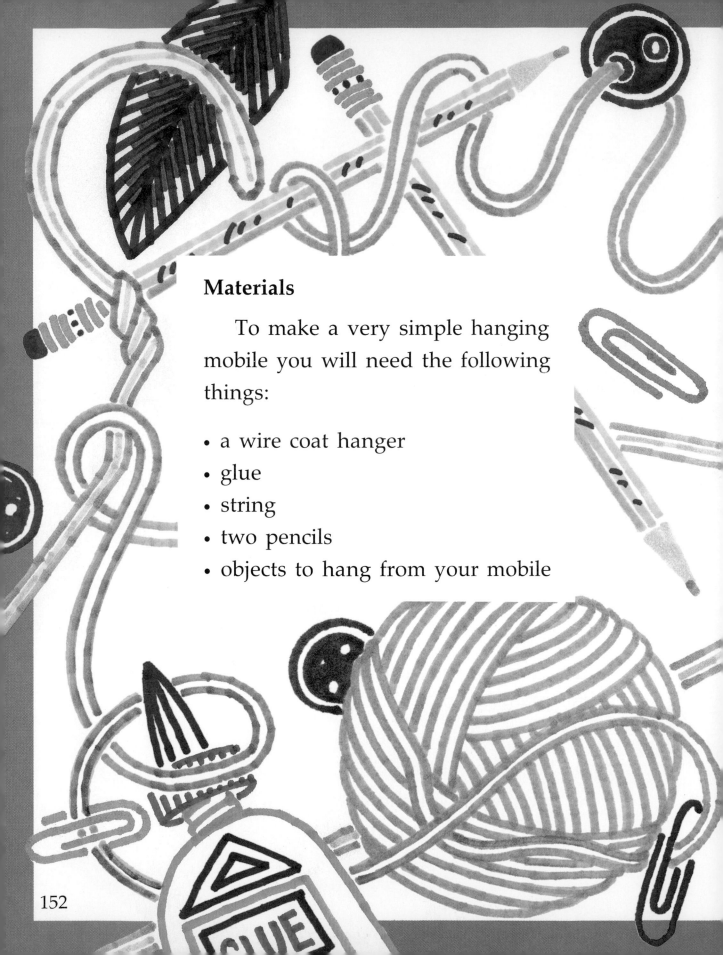

Materials

To make a very simple hanging mobile you will need the following things:

- a wire coat hanger
- glue
- string
- two pencils
- objects to hang from your mobile

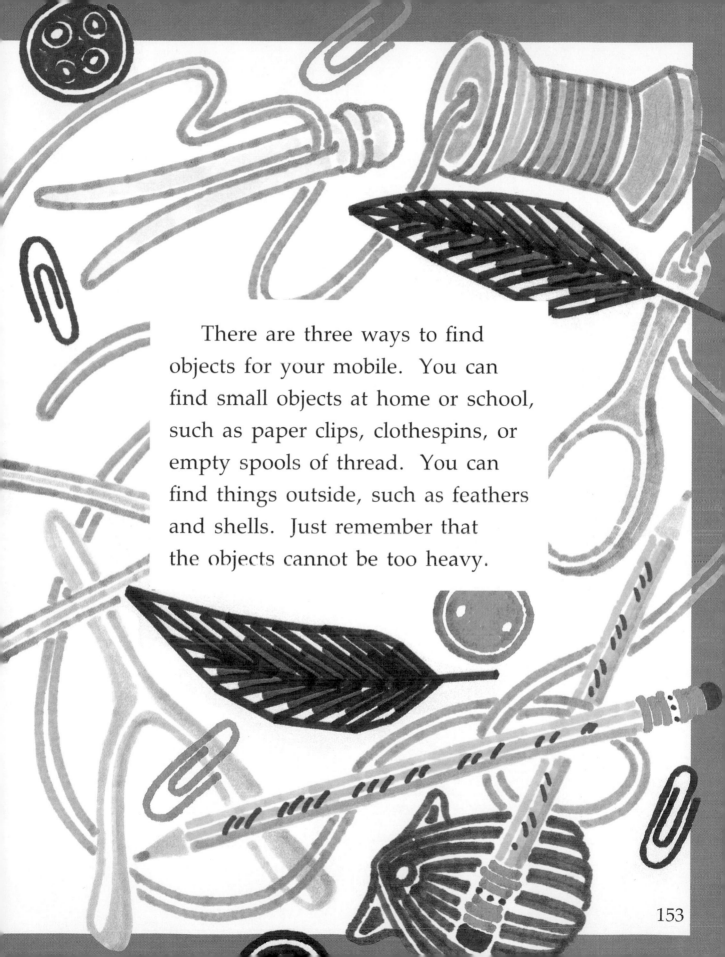

There are three ways to find objects for your mobile. You can find small objects at home or school, such as paper clips, clothespins, or empty spools of thread. You can find things outside, such as feathers and shells. Just remember that the objects cannot be too heavy.

A third way to find objects is to make them. You can do this by cutting out shapes from paper or felt. Make sure you decorate the shapes on both sides. When they turn around on the mobile, both sides will show. You may want to make a fish mobile or a butterfly mobile. These are just two ideas, but you can think of more.

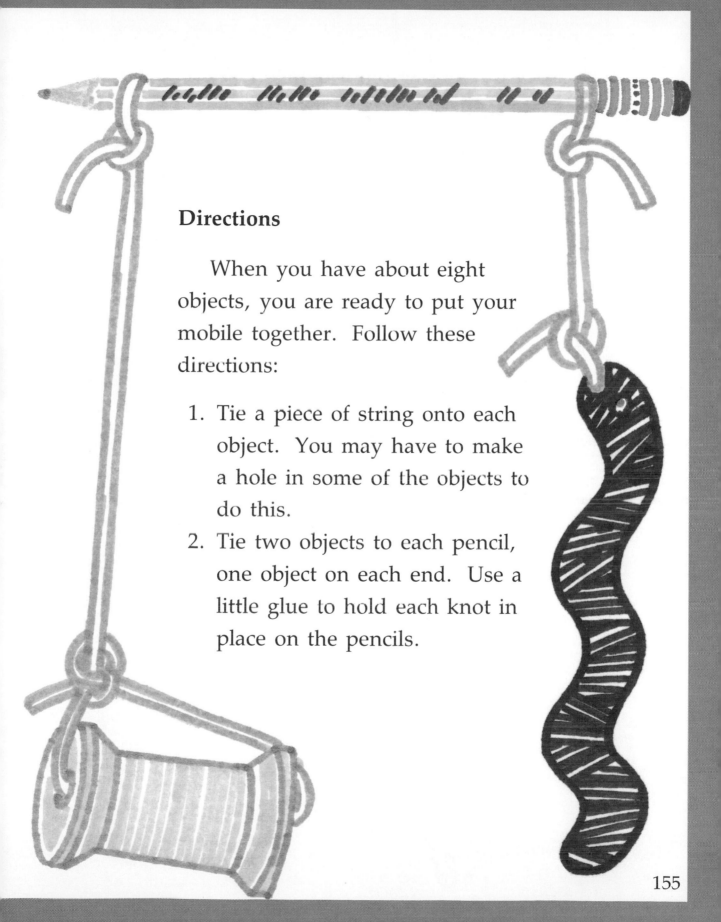

Directions

When you have about eight objects, you are ready to put your mobile together. Follow these directions:

1. Tie a piece of string onto each object. You may have to make a hole in some of the objects to do this.
2. Tie two objects to each pencil, one object on each end. Use a little glue to hold each knot in place on the pencils.

3. Tie a string onto the middle of each pencil.

4. Hold one pencil up by the string and see if the two objects are balanced. If one end of the pencil is up and the other end down, the objects are not balanced. Slide the string you are holding toward the end of the pencil that is down. Then use a little glue to hold the string in place on the pencil.

5. Do the same thing to your second pencil.

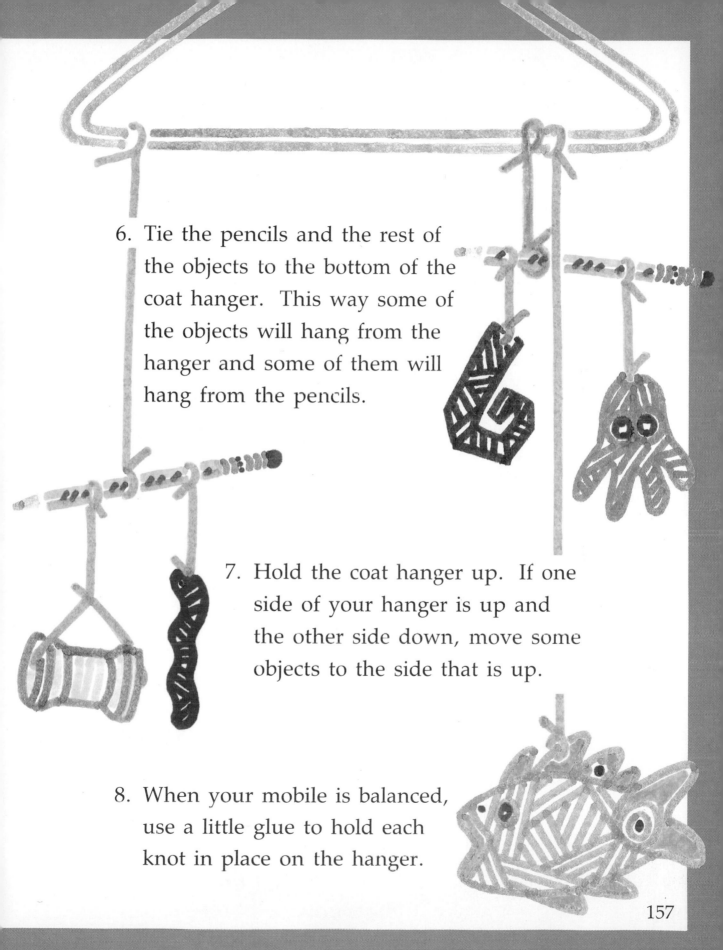

6. Tie the pencils and the rest of the objects to the bottom of the coat hanger. This way some of the objects will hang from the hanger and some of them will hang from the pencils.

7. Hold the coat hanger up. If one side of your hanger is up and the other side down, move some objects to the side that is up.

8. When your mobile is balanced, use a little glue to hold each knot in place on the hanger.

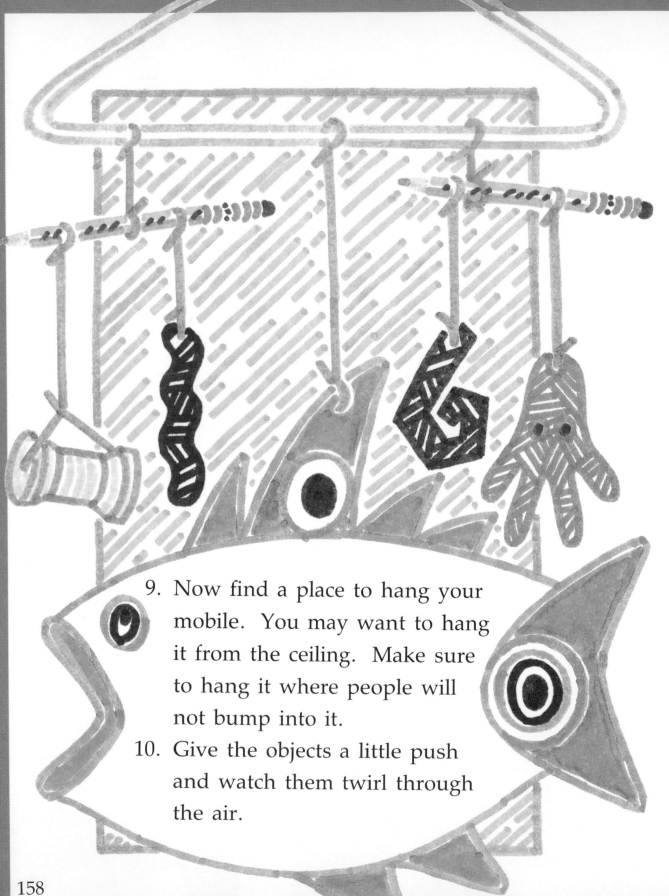

9. Now find a place to hang your mobile. You may want to hang it from the ceiling. Make sure to hang it where people will not bump into it.

10. Give the objects a little push and watch them twirl through the air.

Think About It

1. Why is the word *mobile* a good name for what Alexander Calder invented?
2. Why did Calder want his sculpture to move?
3. What do you do when the objects on a mobile do not balance?
4. What kind of mobile would you like to make?

Create and Share

Make a mobile, using the directions you have just read.

Explore

Read more about Alexander Calder. Share what you learn with your class.

A Perfect Ten

from WONDER WOMEN OF SPORTS
by Betty Millsaps Jones

In 1968 Nadia Comaneci was six years old. She lived in a small town in Romania. One day, a well-known gymnastic coach came to her school. He watched the children playing in the schoolyard.

Nadia and a friend liked to pretend that they were gymnasts. They ran and jumped as they played.

The coach saw Nadia and her friend. He watched them very carefully. When the bell rang, the two girls ran into school.

The coach tried to follow them. He thought that Nadia could become a very good gymnast. He wanted to work with her, but now he could not find her.

The gymnastic coach went into all the classrooms. He wanted to find Nadia and her friend. He went into Nadia's classroom, but he did not see her. He went back into all the rooms. He still could not find the girls that he had seen playing outside.

Then the gymnastic coach had an idea.
He went back into the classrooms again.
He asked, "Who loves gymnastics?" When
he came into Nadia's room, she jumped up
and waved her hand. The coach had found
her at last.

Nadia began going to a special school
for gymnasts. She had to work very hard.
She practiced every day for four hours.

In July 1976, Nadia was only 14, but she had become one of the best gymnasts in the world. Nadia flew from Romania to Canada to be in the Olympics.

The Olympic Games are the best known sports contests around the world. Each country sends its best runners and jumpers. It sends its best swimmers, ball players, and gymnasts, too.

The gymnasts must do many different gymnastic moves. The judges watch to see how hard the moves are. They rate the gymnasts. The highest score is ten (10.00).

It is very hard to get a ten. Judges take away points for mistakes. By 1976, many gymnasts had competed in the Olympics. Not one had ever scored a ten.

Nadia waited for her turn with the other gymnasts. She walked around. She stretched her arms. She stretched her legs. She blew into her hands. She did back flips. She didn't seem to notice the other gymnasts or the big crowd watching them.

Then it was Nadia's turn at the parallel
bars. The two tall bars stand side by side.
One is nearly two feet higher than the other.
Nadia swung from one bar to the other.

She twisted and turned, spinning through the air. Her body became a blur of arms and legs. Nadia swung around and around the bars. Suddenly, Nadia let go of the bars. She soared through the air. She flung her arms high above her as she landed on the floor.

The crowd roared. They knew that they had seen a great gymnast. Nadia waved to the crowd. She smiled. She knew that she had done well.

The crowd grew quiet. They waited for Nadia's scores. The five judges marked their scorecards. Suddenly, the score flashed on the scoreboard. Nadia's score read 1.00.

For a moment, the crowd was very, very quiet. Then, they burst into cheers. They knew that the score was wrong. The scoreboard could go no higher than 9.99. The judges had not given Nadia a 1.00. Nadia had scored a perfect 10.00.

In the Olympics, Nadia won three gold medals. She scored not just one perfect ten. Nadia Comaneci scored **seven** perfect tens!

Think About It

1. What is a *perfect ten* in the Olympics?
2. How did Nadia become such a good gymnast?
3. How are the stories about Margaret and Nadia alike?
4. What kind of balancing are you best at?

Create and Share

Did you ever do anything that could have been called a perfect ten? Write what it was and how you felt about it.

Explore

Look at the pictures in the newspaper to find someone who plays a sport well. What is his or her name? What sport does he or she play?

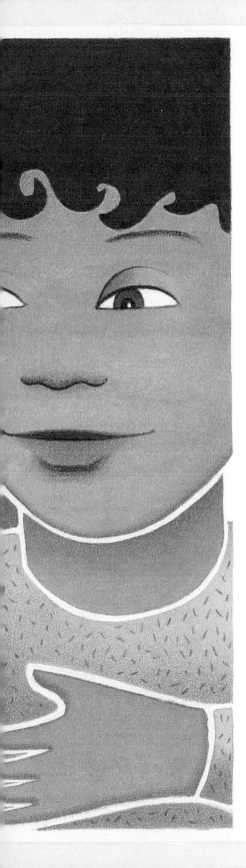

What Are Friends For?

What fun—
To have a friend,
To be a friend,
To make new friends.
What fun!

Jan Hurwitz

Wagon Wheels

by Barbara Brenner

The Dugout

"There it is, boys," Daddy said. "Across this river is Nicodemus, Kansas. That is where we are going to build our house. There is free land for everyone here in the West. All we have to do is go and get it."

We had come a long way to get to Kansas. It had been a hard trip, and a sad one. Mama died on the way. Now there were just the four of us—Daddy, Willie, Little Ben, and me.

"Come on, boys," Daddy called. "Let's put our feet on free dirt."

We crossed the river, wagon and all.

A man was waiting for us on the other side.

"I am Sam Hickman," he said. "Welcome to the town of Nicodemus."

"Why, thank you," Daddy said. "But where *is* your town?"

"Right here," Mr. Hickman said.

We did not see any houses. But we saw smoke coming out of holes in the prairie.

"Holes!" my Daddy said. "Holes in the ground are for rabbits and snakes, not for free black people. I am a carpenter. I can build fine wood houses for this town."

"No time to build wood houses now," Mr. Hickman told my Daddy. "Winter is coming. And winter in Kansas is *mean*. You had better get yourself a dugout before the ground freezes."

Daddy knew Sam Hickman was right. We got our shovels and we dug a dugout. It wasn't much of a place—dirt floor, dirt walls, no windows. The roof was just grass and branches, but we were glad to have that dugout when the wind began to whistle across the prairie.

Every night Willie lit the lamp and
made a fire. I cooked a rabbit stew or fried
a pan of fish fresh from the river. After
supper Daddy would always say, "How
about a song or two?"

He would take out his banjo and
Plink–a–plunk! Plink–a–plunk!

Pretty soon that dugout felt like home.

Indians

Winter came. That Kansas winter *was* mean. It snowed day after day. We could not hunt or fish. We had no more rabbit stew. We had no more fish fresh from the river. All we had was cornmeal mush to eat.

Then one day there was no more cornmeal. There was not a lick of food in the whole town of Nicodemus. There was nothing left to burn for firewood. Little Ben cried all the time. He was so cold and hungry. Daddy wrapped blankets around him.

"Hush, baby son," he said to him. "Try to sleep. The supply train will be coming soon."

But the supply train did not come that day or the next.

On the third day we heard the sound of horses. Daddy looked out to see who it was.

"Oh, no!" he said. "Indians!"

We were *so* scared. We had all heard stories about Indians. I tried to be brave.

We watched from the dugout. Everyone in Nicodemus was watching the Indians.

First they made a circle. Then each Indian took something from his saddlebag and dropped it on the ground. The Indians turned and rode straight toward the dugouts.

"Now they are coming for us!" Willie cried.

But the Indians rode right past us and kept on going.

We waited a long time to be sure they were gone. Then everyone ran out into the snow to see what the Indians had left. It was *food!*

Everyone talked at once.

"Look!"

"Fresh deer meat!"

"Fish!"

"Dried beans and squash!"

"And bundles of sticks to keep our fires burning."

There was a feast in Nicodemus that night. But before we ate, Daddy said to us, "I want you to remember this day. You will be able to tell everyone how the Osage Indians were friends to the people in Nicodemus."

Think About It

1. Who is telling this story?
2. Why has the family come to Nicodemus, Kansas?
3. Why does the family live in a dugout?
4. What act of friendship saves the family's lives?
5. How else is friendship shown in this story?

Create and Share

Write about a time when someone did something special for you.

Explore

Read about the Osage Indians.

The Hare Who Had Many Friends

from ONCE IN A WOOD *by Eve Rice*

The Hare had many, many friends—the Crow, the Goat, and the Cow. Everyone was Hare's good friend, everyone except Fox.

Every time Hare saw Fox, she ran to save her life.

But one day, when Fox came round,
Hare thought, "Why should I run away?
My many friends will help me out!"

Hare went to Crow and said, "Please,
Crow, Fox is coming! Will you hide me in
your tree?"

"Oh," said Crow. "I'd like to help. But
this tree is very small. It cannot hold us
both."

Hare went to Goat and said, "Please, Goat. Fox is coming! Will you butt him with your horns?"

"Hmmmm," said Goat. "I'd like to help, but I am very busy now. I have a lot to do."

Hare went to Cow and said, "Please, Cow. Fox is coming! Will you chase him far away?"

"Ah," said Cow. "I'd like to help, but I cannot chase anyone. I have hurt my leg, you know."

"Yes, I do know," said Hare.

And then with Fox right behind, Hare ran to save her life once more.

"Alas!" she said when she was safe. "Those in trouble soon find out how many friends they really have. I once thought I had so many. Now I see that I was wrong—for, in fact, I haven't any!"

Since Hanna Moved Away

The tires on my bike are flat.
The sky is grouchy gray.
At least it sure feels like that
Since Hanna moved away.

Chocolate ice cream tastes like prunes.
December's come to stay.
They've taken back the Mays and Junes
Since Hanna moved away.

Flowers smell like halibut.
Velvet feels like hay.
Every handsome dog's a mutt
Since Hanna moved away.

Nothing's fun to laugh about.
Nothing's fun to play.
They call me, but I won't come out
Since Hanna moved away.

—Judith Viorst

Think About It

1. Why do you think Crow, Goat, and Cow do not help Hare?
2. What lesson does this story teach?
3. How are the friends in this story different from the friends in "Wagon Wheels"?
4. In the poem "Since Hanna Moved Away," how do you know Hanna's friend is sad?
5. Have you ever had a friend move away? How did you feel?

Create and Share

Write a letter to Hanna's friend. Tell her how to feel better.

Explore

Ask five people what they like best about their friends. Keep a list of what they say.

IZZARD

by Lonzo Anderson

I found a tiny, white lizard egg. I brought it home. I held it in my hand while I took a nap.

Tickle-tickle. I woke up. Something was alive in my hand. I opened my palm. There lay two pieces of eggshell and a tiny, shiny lizard staring at me.

"Oh, look!" I yelled.

My mother looked. "How sweet," she said. "But there are lizards all over the place. We don't need any more."

My father looked. "The heat of your hand made it hatch," he said.

The lizard started to walk. I was afraid it would run away. After a while it ran up my arm. It looked up at me. Then it came up my neck and onto my chin.

"What can I give it to eat?" I wondered.

"Nothing," my father said. "It will know what to do when the time comes to eat."

"May I keep it?"

"You haven't much choice," my father said. "It thinks you are its mother."

"Its *mother!* But I'm a boy!"

My father laughed. "As long as it thinks you are its mother it will stay with you."

"All right," I said. "Then I'll be its mother. Hello, there, Izzard—my daughter, the lizard!"

Izzard was a daytime lizard, so when night came she tried to hide inside my shirt. I put her in my pocket when I went to bed.

My mother said, "Won't you roll on her?"

"Oh, no!" I said. "I'll always know she's there, even when I'm asleep."

In the morning when I woke up the sun was shining. Izzard was sitting on my cheek, looking for her breakfast. She caught a sand fly and ate it.

No one told me I couldn't take her to school, so I did. I soon wished I hadn't.

She sat on top of my head and jumped at flies. She sat on my desk, snapping at whatever bugs came by. I think she was showing off.

The other children in the school did not listen to the teacher. They watched little Izzard and laughed.

"Jamie," the teacher said, "you will have to get rid of that lizard."

"I can't," I said. "I'm its mother."

That was the wrong thing to say. Everybody giggled and the teacher looked angry.

"Jamie, give it to me," she said. "I'll keep it in my desk until after school." She held out her hand.

Izzard hid inside my shirt.

The teacher stamped her foot. Izzard peeked out from under my chin at her.

She laughed. She couldn't help it, I could tell.

From then on I had to leave Izzard at home. She hated that, but she could not follow me because I walked too fast for her.

As soon as I came home she would run to meet me.

When I played with my friends, Izzard liked to go with me. She would stay in my shirt pocket. She hung on for dear life sometimes, but always with at least one eye sticking out to keep track of what was going on.

The more I watched her and thought about it, the more I believed that Izzard didn't know that she was a lizard. There are lizards all over the island, but she didn't seem to like them. She liked only me.

"I'll bet she thinks she's a person, like me," I said.

"I'll bet she does," my mother agreed.

In June, while Izzard was still young, my parents took my sister and me on a long trip. We went to visit my grandmother for the summer. Izzard was not allowed to go with me.

I worried about her. Would she forget me? Would she be okay without me?

We came home in the fall in time for school. Izzard was nowhere to be found. I felt sad and lonely when I went to bed.

In the morning, as soon as it was light, *plop!*—there was Izzard. She danced. She jumped. She looked into my eyes and ran away and back again.

I knew she was trying to say, "I'm so glad to see you! Where have you been?"

One day when I came home from school Izzard was nowhere in the house. It was daytime, so I knew she was not sleeping somewhere.

I went out the back door and looked.
There she was, six feet up on a palm tree.

She started running down the tree to
come to me.

Just then I saw a mongoose under a big
leaf nearby. It was waiting to catch a
lizard.

I yelled, "Izzard, no!"

She couldn't understand. She came on.
The mongoose was very fast. He jumped
at Izzard. Izzard was even quicker. She
jumped straight up into the air. She came
down right on top of the mongoose's head!

Before the mongoose knew what had
happened, Izzard was off again. She got to
me just as I was chasing the mongoose
away.

Izzard ran up my leg and inside my
shirt. She would not come out for a long
time.

Soon after that Izzard found out she was a lizard and not a person. A male lizard came near me to catch a bug. Izzard was jealous. She jumped at him.

When he left, she followed him a little way. Then she came back to look at me again.

I put out my hand to pick her up. She jumped back.

She wouldn't let me pick her up!

Izzard afraid of *me?* I couldn't believe it. I was hurt.

"She's a grown-up lizard now," my father said.

Summer came again, and once more we went to visit my grandmother.

We came back in the fall. As soon as we came into the house, Izzard came to me.

She ran onto my hand and I raised her in front of my face. She stared into my eyes, first with one eye, then with the other, and wriggled. It was like old times. Izzard was still my very good friend. But she didn't stay with me. She would visit me often, but she lived with the other lizards.

Guess what I found on my pillow last night when I went to bed. A lizard egg!

Do you think it is Izzard's—a special present just for me?

Think About It

1. Why do you think Izzard likes Jamie so much?
2. After Izzard grows up, why doesn't she live with Jamie anymore?
3. Do you think Izzard really leaves the egg as a special present for Jamie? Why or why not?
4. Would you like to have a pet lizard? Why or why not?

Create and Share

Write what you think happens to the egg that Jamie finds at the end of the story.

Explore

Read a story about a friendship between an animal and a person.

Be Yourself

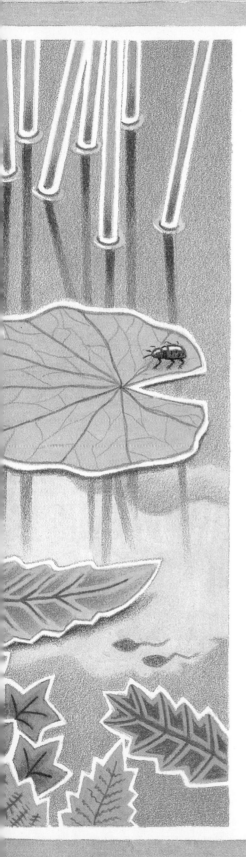

In the mirror
I can see
Lots of things
But mostly—me.

REFLECTION
by Myra Cohn Livingston

WHAT MAKES YOU

THE WAY YOU LOOK

DIFFERENT?

THE CLOTHES YOU WEAR

WHAT MAKES YOU

DIFFERENT ?

THE THINGS YOU LIKE TO DO

WHAT MAKES YOU

DIFFERENT?

Just Me

Nobody sees what I can see,
For back of my eyes there is only me.
And nobody knows how my thoughts begin,
For there's only myself inside my skin.
Isn't it strange how everyone owns
Just enough skin to cover his bones?
My father's would be too big to fit—
I'd be all wrinkled inside of it.
And my baby brother's is much too small—
It just wouldn't cover me up at all.
But I feel just right in the skin I wear,
And there's nobody like me anywhere.

—*Margaret Hillert*

Arthur's Eyes

by Marc Brown

This is Arthur before he got glasses. He looked fine, but he couldn't see very well. Sometimes he got headaches.

Arthur had to hold his book so close that his nose got in the way. He couldn't see the board. Francine had to read Arthur the problems.

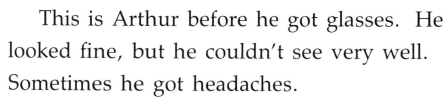

"Can't you see?" she always asked.

Francine got every problem right.
Arthur didn't.

No one wanted to play with Arthur.

Arthur's father and mother took him to
the optometrist. Dr. Iris tested Arthur's
eyes.

"You need glasses," said Dr. Iris.

Arthur tried on all kinds of frames. He
chose the ones he liked best.

"You look very handsome in your new
glasses," said his father.

"Everything looks clearer," said Arthur.

His mother told him he looked very smart.

But the next morning his friends laughed at him. Francine called him names.

None of Arthur's friends wore glasses. No one in his family wore glasses, either. Arthur felt awful.

He didn't care if he could see. Arthur decided he would lose his glasses.

Arthur put his shirt in the laundry. In the front pocket were his glasses. His mother found them the next morning.

"You have to be more careful, Arthur. You're lucky they weren't broken."

That day at school, Arthur hid his glasses in his lunchbox. He told his teacher he forgot them.

But now things were harder to see than ever. When Arthur walked down the hall to the boys' room he had to count the doors. He opened the door. Francine was talking. What was Francine doing in the boys' room?

"Get out of here!" screamed Francine. "This is the girls' room!"

Arthur bumped into the wall. He couldn't find the door. Now all the girls were screaming.

Out in the hall, doors opened. Teachers ran out. The principal ran out too. Everyone was looking at Arthur. Arthur turned red. He wanted to hide. The principal took Arthur to his office.

Then Arthur's teacher talked to him.

"Why don't you keep your glasses in a case in your pocket, as I do?" he asked.

"You wear glasses?" asked Arthur.

"Yes, for reading," said his teacher.

He took them out. They looked just like Arthur's. Suddenly Arthur felt better.

He went to his lunchbox and put on his glasses. In gym Arthur made ten baskets. Francine made four.

That afternoon Arthur didn't need
Francine to read the problems on the
board. He got every one right. Arthur
could see Francine's paper. She missed
two. After school Francine asked Arthur to
be on her team.

"I'll think about it," said Arthur.

The next morning Arthur was very
surprised when he saw Francine.

"They're my movie star glasses," said
Francine.

"But there isn't any glass in them," said
Arthur.

"It doesn't matter. They help me think
harder and make me look beautiful," said
Francine.

That afternoon a photographer took the class picture.

"Just a minute," said Arthur.

He took out his glasses. He carefully polished them and put them on.

"Everyone ready?" asked the photographer.

"Wait!" said Francine.

She ran to get her purse. She took out her movie star glasses.

"Okay, I'm ready too!" said Francine.

"Smile!" said the photographer.

Think About It

1. Why doesn't Arthur want to wear his new glasses?
2. How might the poem "Just Me" and the photo essay "What Makes You Different?" have helped Arthur when he first got his glasses?
3. Think of a time when you had to wear something you did not want to wear. How did you feel?

Create and Share

If you wear glasses, write about the time when you got glasses. If you don't wear glasses, find someone who does. Ask the person how he or she felt about getting glasses.

Explore

Read another book by Marc Brown.

Butterfly Wings

How would it be
on a day in June
to open your eyes
in a dark cocoon,

And soften one end
and crawl outside,
and find you had wings
to open wide,

And find you could fly
to a bush or tree
or float on the air
like a boat at sea . . .

How would it be?

—by Aileen Fisher

220

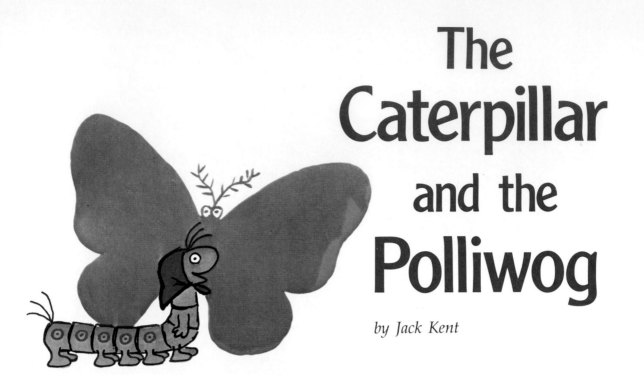

The Caterpillar and the Polliwog

by Jack Kent

Caterpillars aren't like other folks. As ducks and hippopotamuses and you and I get older, we get bigger.

But not caterpillars. They turn into butterflies.

Turning into something else like that is not a thing just anybody can do.

Down by the pond there lived a caterpillar who was very proud of being different. She bragged about it to her friends.

"When I grow up, I'm going to turn into something else," she told the snail.

"That's nice," said the snail, who really didn't care one way or the other.

"When I grow up, I'm going to turn into something else," she told the turtle.

"I don't blame you," said the turtle, who didn't much like wiggly things.

"When I grow up, I'm going to turn into something else," she told the polliwog.

"What fun!" said the polliwog. "What are you going to turn into?"

But the caterpillar hurried on her way, looking for someone else to tell her secret to.

"I wish *I* could turn into something else when I grow up!" said the polliwog.

"You *will*," said the fish. "*All* polliwogs do."

"What am I going to turn into?" the polliwog asked.

But the fish saw a tasty bug and dashed after it.

"When I grow up," said the caterpillar, who had circled the pond and was going around for the second time, "when I grow up," she told the polliwog again, "I'm going to turn into something else."

"So am *I!*" said the polliwog.

"*You?!*" The caterpillar was so surprised she almost fell into the pond.

"The fish said so," the polliwog told her. "Fish know things. They go to school."

The caterpillar was upset.

"I thought only caterpillars could do it," she said rather sadly.

"What are we going to turn into?" the polliwog asked.

"Well, *I'm* going to turn into a *butterfly!*" said the caterpillar.

"Then I guess I will, too!" the polliwog said happily. "What fun! Let's do it together!"

"All right," the caterpillar agreed, although she would rather have done it alone. "But I get to go first!"

The polliwog didn't mind. He wasn't at all sure how it was done. "I'll watch you," he said.

So when the time came, the caterpillar started to spin a cocoon.

"This is the tricky part," she said.

The polliwog watched as the caterpillar spun. Soon only her head was uncovered.

"Now I have to close the lid," she said. "And when I come out, I'll be a butterfly."

"Go ahead!" the polliwog said excitedly. "I want to see you do it!"

"It will take a while," the caterpillar warned. She started spinning again and was soon out of sight in the cocoon.

For a long time nothing happened. But the polliwog waited.

He watched and watched and watched, for days and days and days.

At last there was activity in the cocoon. The end of it opened and, very slowly, the caterpillar climbed out. Only she wasn't a caterpillar anymore. She was a *butterfly!* A beautiful yellow butterfly!

The polliwog was so excited he hopped up and down with delight! He *hopped!* Up and down! Like a *frog!*

"I was so busy watching *you*," he said, "I didn't notice what was happening to *me!*"

"You're a very handsome frog," the butterfly said, as she flew off to try her new wings.

But the frog was puzzled. "I thought I was going to be a butterfly," he said.

A caterpillar wiggled by.

"When I grow up," he said proudly to the frog, "I'm going to turn into something else!"

But the frog wasn't listening. He was admiring his reflection in the water.

"I *am*, you know, a *very* handsome frog!" he said.

Tricksters

Tracey Trickster has some fun
    playing tricks on *everyone*.
Why does Tracey look so grim?
    Someone played a trick on *him*!

Barbara Schmidt

The Fox and the Goat

from ONCE IN A WOOD *by Eve Rice*

Fox went walking in the woods and fell into a well.

"This well is very deep," Fox thought sadly to himself. "I cannot jump very high. How will I get out again?"

Just then a thirsty goat passed by.

"Hello, Fox," said the goat. "Why are you down in the well?"

"Oh, Goat," replied clever Fox, "I came to get a drink, of course. This water is the finest in the wood."

"It is?" asked Goat.

"It is!" said Fox. "Come and taste it for yourself. I'm sure you will agree."

Goat jumped down into the well. When Goat had had a drink, he said, "This water is as sweet as it can be. But tell me, Fox, how will we get out again?"

"That is easy," said the fox. "If you will
stand very still, I can climb upon your back.
As soon as I am out, I will pull you up."

So Goat stood still and Fox climbed out.
Then Fox turned and walked away.

"Oh, please!" Goat called to Fox.
"Don't go! How will I get out again?"

"Don't ask me," the fox replied. "You
should have looked before you leaped—
and asked yourself the question then."

Think About It

1. Why does Fox trick Goat?
2. How could Fox have gotten out of the well without tricking Goat?
3. Whom would you rather have as a friend, Fox or Goat? Why?
4. What does the saying "Look before you leap" mean?
5. Do you feel sorry for Goat? Why or why not?

Create and Share

Think of a way Goat can get out of the well. Write a new ending for the story.

Explore

Read a story about a fox. Does the fox play any clever tricks?

The GANG and MRS. HIGGINS

by George Shannon

Many years ago, pioneers came to Kansas. They settled on the flat grassy plains.

Some of them were good people, and some were not. Mr. and Mrs. Higgins were among the best. They came to Kansas from Ohio.

Together they built two houses. The first was made of sod. Three years later they built a wooden house.

They set up a trading post. Mrs. Higgins ran the store while Mr. Higgins worked the fields.

The land around them was flat. Mr. and Mrs. Higgins could look for miles before they saw any hills.

Mrs. Higgins cooked food for anyone who came to her door. When Mr. Higgins was not busy in the fields, he helped lead new settlers across the plains.

The meanest settlers in Kansas were the Anderson brothers. They were the nastiest gang of robbers west of the Missouri River. All five Anderson brothers lived in a crumbling sod hut. It had more cracks than it had windows.

Each of the Anderson brothers owned one set of clothes. They kept themselves and their clothes clean by swimming in the river. But they liked to swim only when the river was warm. Their last bath every year was in September. It had to last until spring.

The gang was always hungry. The only meal they could cook was beans and beef jerky. If they wanted any good food, they had to find it where they robbed.

Robbing settlers was better than robbing banks. Banks had only money. Settlers sometimes had money, but they always had food.

Each morning when Mr. Higgins left to work in the fields, he said to his wife, "Be careful, and watch out for the Anderson gang."

Each morning Mrs. Higgins replied, "I'll be fine. Don't worry."

Days and months passed and only
settlers stopped by the Higgins house.

Then one hot August morning Mrs.
Higgins saw the gang riding in from the
river. She was just starting to do the
laundry under her shade tree. Mrs.
Higgins was alone. The gang rode up
yelling and shooting in the air.

"Fix us some dinner!" the gang yelled.

Mrs. Higgins kept on washing. They yelled again. Mrs. Higgins stopped washing and smiled.

"Dinner will be ready before you can wash up at the well," she said.

"We don't wash," the gang said. They followed her into the kitchen.

Mrs. Higgins had made a big batch of biscuits and gravy. She started to say, "Come and get it," but the gang was already racing to the table like a herd of buffalo.

She served the food. Then she gathered up more clothes and went back to her washing.

Those robbers stuffed biscuits into their mouths as fast as they could. When they were done, they walked out to the shade tree.

"This is a trading post," said the oldest, "so you must have gold. Where is it?"

"We don't have any," said Mrs. Higgins, and she kept on washing clothes.

"Every trading post has gold!" said the youngest. "If you won't tell us where it is, we'll just find it ourselves."

The gang emptied the cupboards, the barrels and the trunks. They dumped out the dressers, and tore open the beds. But they could find no gold. The more they searched, the madder they got.

Mrs. Higgins never looked up. She just kept on washing. The Andersons were getting more and more angry.

"You have one more chance," yelled the tallest. "Tell us where the gold is and you won't get hurt."

"I told you there was no gold," Mrs. Higgins said, and she kept on washing. "You can go ahead and shoot me, but there still won't be any gold."

The gang did not know what to do. They couldn't find any gold. Maybe there wasn't any. They fussed and cussed, but at last they decided to give up the search.

They got on their horses and rode off in a cloud of dust.

When Mr. Higgins returned, Mrs. Higgins was still washing.

"You should have been here this morning!" she told him. "The Anderson gang came hunting for gold."

"Are you all right?" he asked.

"Of course," she said. "But they tore up the house."

"Did they get the gold?" Mr. Higgins wanted to know.

Mrs. Higgins smiled and shook her head. Then she stuck her hands back into the washtub, and pulled out a very wet and very clean bag of gold.

Think About It

1. How does Mrs. Higgins trick the Anderson gang?
2. Why was the washtub a good spot to hide the gold?
3. Do you think Mrs. Higgins was afraid of the Anderson gang? Why or why not?
4. How is this trick different from the trick in "The Fox and the Goat"?

Create and Share

Write about another trick Mrs. Higgins plays on the Anderson gang the next time they come.

Explore

Locate Kansas and Ohio on the map.

Nobody Comes to Dinner

by F. Emerson Andrews

Oscar was having a bad day. The alarm didn't go off, so he got up late. He couldn't find his favorite blue sneakers, and after a long search he remembered he must have left them in the yard. But it was raining and they would be soaked. Oscar had to put on his black cowboy boots. When he got to school, the boys and girls pointed to his big boots and giggled.

After school was even worse. Oscar went over to his friends' house, but they said, "Go away. We're playing and we don't want you."

He went home and waited for a telephone call, but nobody called. He went down to the playground, but sitting alone on the swings in the rain is no fun.

Now it was dinner time. Oscar was
mad and decided he was not going to eat.
He told that to his mother firmly. His
mother took him by the hand and pulled
him to the table. His older sister Jane was
already there and little Christopher was
sitting in his chair with the pillow on it.

His mother came in, carrying a tray
with three bowls of steaming soup.

"It's good vegetable soup tonight," she
said, "the kind you all like."

"I hate vegetable soup," said Oscar as
his bowl was placed before him. "I hate all
vegetables."

"Just try a little," said his mother.

Oscar closed his lips and screwed up his
face. "I don't like you."

Jane reached over and took the spoon.

"Come on now, Oscar."

"I don't like you either. I don't like
Christopher. I like nobody."

Everyone at the table looked at Oscar.
He glared back.

251

"Well," said Jane, after a moment, "that's the first nice thing you've said today. You *do* like Nobody. Just a minute, and I'll call him in."

She opened an imaginary door, and said, "Do come in, Mr. Nobody. Oscar says he likes you. Please have dinner with us."

She drew up a chair.

"There, Nobody, I hope you're comfortable. I'm Jane, and at your left is our little brother, Christopher. Across the table is Oscar, who just said he likes Nobody."

"Stop being silly," growled Oscar. "I don't see anybody."

"If you look carefully," said Jane, "you will see Nobody is sitting between Christopher and me."

What she said was true, and Oscar almost grinned. Jane was up to one of her games again, and sometimes they were fun. Without knowing it, he picked up his spoon and began to eat his soup.

"Good!" said Jane. "When you have emptied your soup bowl, pass it over. Nobody likes to get empty soup bowls."

When it was almost time for dessert Jane began asking about birthdays.

"My birthday is on July fifth," she said. "When's yours, Oscar?"

"April second."

"Oh, yes. You're almost an April Fool, aren't you? And how about Christopher? I think it's September something."

Their mother had heard their questions and came to the doorway to answer.

"Christopher's is September eighth," she said.

"Just what I thought!" said Jane. "Today is Nobody's birthday."

"Happy birthday, Nobody!" Oscar shouted.

Then their mother went into the kitchen. A few minutes later she came to the kitchen doorway. "I baked a cake this afternoon. I was going to ask if you all wanted cake and ice cream. We could give Nobody the cake for his birthday. But I looked everywhere, and we are fresh out of birthday candles."

"Why Mother," said Jane, "of course
Nobody wants a birthday cake with no
candles!"

"Of course," said their mother. "Why
didn't I know that?"

"Anyway," added Oscar, "we wouldn't
know how many candles to put on. How
old is Nobody? Can anybody answer me that?"

In a minute Jane had the answer.

"But of course. Nobody knows how old
he is."

At this moment their mother came in,
with the cake.

They all sang "Happy Birthday" to Nobody.

And Nobody didn't like the cake.

Think About It

1. Why was Oscar having a bad day?
2. How does Jane help Oscar?
3. Do you like the way the family helped Oscar feel better? Why or why not?
4. Have you ever used a trick to help someone feel better? Explain what you did.

Create and Share

Make up your own funny sentences about Nobody.

Explore

Ask other people what they have done to help a friend feel better. Make a list of their ideas. Then use them someday.

The Emperor's New Clothes

retold by Stephen Krensky

A long time ago there was an emperor who loved to wear beautiful clothes. He was always buying new robes and belts and hats and coats. The emperor had different clothes for every day. He got dressed and undressed a lot.

One day two men came to the emperor's town. They told everyone they were weavers.

"We weave very beautiful cloth," said one of the men.

"Our cloth is very special too," said the other. "It is invisible to anyone who is foolish."

The emperor soon heard about the two weavers. "They must make me some clothes," he said. "Then I will know who is smart and who is foolish."

The weavers asked for silk and gold thread to make the emperor's new clothes. The emperor gave them the best silk and gold thread he had.

The weavers never used them. They hid the silk and gold thread in their bags. Then they sat before their loom, pretending to weave.

After a week, the emperor got curious.

"I wonder how the weavers are doing," he thought. "I will send my prime minister to see them."

The prime minister went to see the weavers at once.

"Come in," they said. "Our work is going very well."

They pointed to the loom.

The prime minister gasped. "I see no cloth," he thought. "If foolish people cannot see the cloth, does this mean I am foolish?" He opened his eyes wide. He rubbed them. It didn't help. He still couldn't see a thing.

"This is terrible," he thought. "Nobody must find out I am foolish."

"Do you like the colors?" the weavers asked.

"Lovely," said the prime minister. "I've never seen anything like them."

He went back to the palace and told the emperor the cloth was beautiful. The emperor was pleased.

When another week had passed, the emperor got curious again. This time he sent the lord chamberlain to see how the weavers were doing.

The weavers were glad to see him. "Come in," they said proudly. "Take a good look."

The lord chamberlain stared and stared. Like the prime minister, he didn't see a thing.

"Am I so foolish?" thought the lord chamberlain. "Oh, dear. No one must find out."

"So what do you think?" the weavers asked.

"Oh, my," said the lord chamberlain. "Everything seems to be going very well."

And that's what he told the emperor.

Everyone in town was soon talking about the wonderful cloth the weavers were making. People talked about it in the shops. They talked about it at home. Some people even talked about it in their sleep.

After three weeks, the emperor came to see the cloth for himself. The prime minister and the lord chamberlain went with him.

The weavers were working at the loom.

"Please come in, Your Majesty," said one weaver.

The other weaver pointed to the loom. "We are very proud of this part," he said.

"Ah, yes," the prime minister said quickly.

"Splendid!" cried the lord chamberlain.

The emperor was shocked. What were they talking about? He could not see any cloth. "Does this mean I am a foolish person?" he wondered. "This must stay my secret."

"Is anything wrong, Your Majesty?" the weavers asked.

"No, no," said the emperor. "Of course, nothing's wrong. I'm very happy. I want to wear the clothes in the parade tomorrow. Will they be ready?"

"We will do our best," they said.

That night the two weavers didn't sleep at all. They were very busy finishing the emperor's new clothes. They pretended to take the cloth off the loom. They pretended to cut it into pieces. They pretended to sew the pieces together.

Just before sunrise they said they were done.

The emperor soon came to get dressed. The weavers lifted their arms, pretending to hold something in their hands.

"These are the pants," said one of the weavers. "And this is the robe. They are very light. You will almost feel as though you are wearing nothing at all."

The weavers pretended to lift each piece of clothing and place it on the emperor.

"Notice the buttons," said one weaver.

"And the lace edge," said the other.

"Oh, yes," said the emperor. "Splendid work."

Finally they were done. The weavers stood back and clapped their hands.

The emperor stood in front of the mirror looking at himself.

"A perfect fit!" he said.

The lord chamberlain knocked at the door. "Is the emperor ready to start the parade?" he asked.

The emperor took another look in the mirror. "They are handsome clothes, aren't they?" he said. Then he went out.

The emperor led the parade up and
down the streets of the town. Everyone
came out to watch. All the people knew
the story of the emperor's clothes. They all
pretended to see them.

"Did you ever see such clothes?"

"What a wonderful fit!"

Nobody was willing to say that the
clothes couldn't be seen. Nobody wanted
to be thought foolish by anyone else.

One little girl looked at the emperor and laughed. "He doesn't have anything on!" she cried.

Many people heard her. They whispered to themselves, repeating what the girl had said.

"She's right, you know."

"He doesn't have anything on."

"He has nothing on at all!" the people shouted together.

The emperor bit his lip. He knew they were right, but he was not going to let them know it. "I must keep going," he thought. So he kept walking as proudly as he could. The laughter of the crowd followed him all the way back to the palace.

Think About It

1. Why does the emperor believe the weavers?
2. Why do the weavers trick the emperor?
3. Think about all the tricks played in TRICKSTERS. What bad or good thing happens in each story because a trick is played?
4. Do you think it is right to play tricks on people? Explain your answer.

Create and Share

Write about the kind of lesson the emperor learns in this story.

Explore

Read another Andersen fairy tale.

Glossary

A

aboard on a ship, boat, bus, or plane (The boat cannot leave until everyone is *aboard*.)

acorn the seed of an oak tree (The *acorns* are small and brown and look like they have little caps on them.)

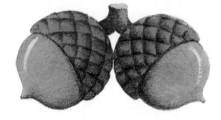

against in contact with (The snow is so deep that it is piled *against* the door.)

agree to think the same thing (Maria and I *agree* that apples are very good to eat.) **agreed, agreeing**

airplane a flying machine with wings (Most birds cannot fly as high as an *airplane* can.)

alive living; not dead (That flower in the garden is *alive*, but the one in the vase is dead.)

allergic having an allergy (See **allergy**.) (Dog hair makes me sneeze because I am *allergic* to it.)

allergy a sickness in which a person sneezes, coughs, or itches when close to a certain kind of food, hair, or plant (When I drink milk, I itch all over because of my *allergy*.) *pl.* **allergies**

allow to let (My mom *allows* me to watch TV if I do my homework first.)

among **1.** one of; part of (Jamie was *among* the many children at the game.) **2.** in between (Butterflies are flying *among* the flowers.)

ancient of a time that was long, long ago (Most things made in *ancient* times are gone by now.)

answer to say something when someone asks you a question (Mary asked me where I had found her glasses, and I *answered* that I had found them under the chair.)

arrive to come to a place (If you want to get a good seat at the game, you must *arrive* early.) **arrived, arriving**

automobile a car (Most *automobiles* need gas to run.)

B

balance to make or keep steady so something does not fall (Can you *balance* a book on your head, or does it fall off?) **balanced, balancing**

ballplayer someone who plays in a ball game

barrel a large, round, wooden container that is flat on the top and bottom (The *barrel* was full of water.)

baseball a game played by two teams with nine players each. A player tries to hit a ball with a bat, and then run and touch four bases.

beautifully in a way that is very pretty or good (Bill sang the song *beautifully*.)

between in a time or space that separates two things (April is the month *between* March and May.)

bicycle something to ride on, with two wheels and a seat (You push two pedals with your feet to make a *bicycle* move.)

birthday the day of the year a person was born on (Rico's *birthday* is May 1.)

buffalo a big animal that is something like a cow with a shaggy head (A cow is smaller than a *buffalo*.) *pl.* **buffaloes**

build to make by putting things together (You need wood and nails to *build* a tree house.) **built, building**

built See **build**.

bundle things tied together (We tied 25 newspapers together in a *bundle* for the paper drive.)

C

carefully in a way that is filled with care or thought (Wash that glass *carefully*, or it might break.)

carnival a place with shows and games where you pay money to do things (I went down a water slide at the *carnival*.)

carpenter someone who builds things from wood (The *carpenter* made a toy box.)

carrot a long, thin, orange vegetable (Both people and rabbits like to eat *carrots*.)

castle a very large home with thick stone walls and towers (The king lived in a *castle*.)

cellar the room in a house that is under the ground or on the bottom (In the winter, I keep my bike in our *cellar*.)

choice the act of picking something out; the act of choosing (What is your *choice* of drink, milk or water?)

chopsticks thin sticks, about 12 inches long, used to eat food with (Mr. Chung showed me how to hold two *chopsticks* in one hand and pick up food between them.)

clever   smart; bright (*Clever* people have good ideas.)

clothing   the clothes a person wears (In the winter, thick *clothing* keeps you warm.)

comb   a small tool with little teeth used to smooth or untangle your hair (Jim used his *comb* to make a part in his hair.)

comfortable   feeling good, with no pain (The big soft chair made me feel *comfortable*.)

compete   to try to win (Runners *compete* in a race.) **competed, competing**

contest   a game or race to see who will win (We had a *contest* to see who could throw the ball farthest.)

cottage   a little house (Uncle William's *cottage* has a big maple tree in front of it.)

cupboard   a place with doors and shelves for keeping such things as dishes and food (You will find a box of crackers in the *cupboard*.)

D

dangerous   not safe (Playing with matches is *dangerous*.)

daughter   a girl child (Every girl is the *daughter* of her mother and father.)

direct   straight; without being stopped or blocked (The fox ran across the field in a *direct* line.)

directions   the words that tell you how to do something (To put the toy together, you must read the *directions*.)

dollar   a piece of paper money that is worth 100 pennies (Alison bought a big silver balloon for one *dollar*.)

domino   a small game piece that is flat on all sides and has dots on it (Match the dots on your *domino* with mine.) *pl.* **dominoes**

dugout a home made by digging into the side of a hill (The *dugout* had no windows, but it had a door.)

E

eager wanting something very much (The hungry man was *eager* for food.)

early before the usual time; before the time something was supposed to happen (Betty woke up *early* this morning, before the alarm clock rang.) **earlier, earliest**

earn to get something, such as money, for working (Jimmy washes dishes and *earns* two dollars every week.)

easily in an easy way; with no trouble (Jill learned to tie her shoes *easily*, but Kim found it hard.)

either **1.** also (I do not like eggplant; my dad doesn't like it *either*.) **2.** one or the other (You must eat *either* corn or carrots with your meal.)

emperor someone who rules over many people and lands (That *emperor* is richer than any king.)

empty with nothing in it (When a glass is *empty*, you can turn it upside down, and nothing will fall out.) **emptier, emptiest**

enemy something or someone who tries to hurt another (The cat is the *enemy* of the mouse.) *pl.* **enemies**

envelope a folded and closed piece of paper that is used for putting letters in (The birthday card was too big to fit in the *envelope*.)

except but; other than (Everyone is ready to leave *except* Uncle Ted.)

excited   having a lot of eager feeling; stirred up   (The chance to go on a trip around the world would make most people feel *excited*.)

F

famous   well-known; known to many people (That park is *famous* for its flowers.)

fingernail   the hard, bony part at the tip of a finger   (When I have to wait for my sister, I tap on the table with my *fingernails*.)

fisherman   someone whose job is to catch fish and sell them (The *fisherman* is very happy when he catches many fish.) *pl.* **fishermen**

flounder   a very flat ocean fish that is good to eat   (We had *flounder* for dinner last night.)

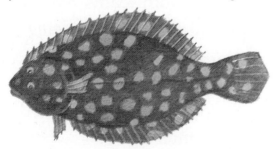

G

gangway   a saying that means "Get out of my way!"   (The man carrying the trunk yelled *Gangway!* so that the crowd would move aside.)

gently   in a soft, tender way (Touch the flower *gently*, or you may hurt it.)

glove   a kind of clothing that you wear on your hand, usually to keep it warm (Mittens do not have a place for each finger in them, but *gloves* do.)

glue   stuff you use to stick things together   (Envelopes are held shut with *glue*.)

guitar   an instrument that makes music when you strum its strings   (The boy played soft music on his *guitar*.)

gym   a place where people play games and train for sports   (The mats in the *gym* are for tumbling.)

gymnast someone who does gymnastics (See **gymnastics.**) (The *gymnast* flipped in the air, and then she landed gracefully on the floor.)

gymnastics exercises that work your muscles and that you do to be strong and fit (Hand stands, back flips, tumbling, and cartwheels are all *gymnastics*.)

H

hamster a furry animal that looks like a large mouse. Most hamsters have a short tail. (Some *hamsters* can live in cages and make good little pets.)

headache a pain in the head (It hurts to try to read when I have a *headache*.)

hermit crab a small sea animal that lives inside a shell left by another animal (Joe could not see the *hermit crab* because it was hiding inside its shell.)

historian someone who writes about the past (The book about the Pilgrims was written by a *historian*.)

hooray See **hurray.**

hurray a shout or cheer that shows happiness (When our team won the game, we shouted *Hurray! Hurray!*)

I

imaginary not real; made up (Sal's *imaginary* friend can walk up the walls.)

inning one round in a baseball game (Both teams have a turn at bat in each *inning*.)

instrument a thing used to do something (A flute and a piano are *instruments* used to make music.)

invent to make something for the first time (Who *invented* the airplane?)

invention something new that someone has made for the first time (Before the *invention* of the airplane, people could not fly.)

invisible not seen; not able to be seen (The glass doors were so clean that they were almost *invisible*.)

island a piece of land with water on all sides (We can get to the *island* in my boat.)

J

jealous 1. afraid that someone you like might like another person better than you (When I saw my best friend playing with that other girl, I felt *jealous*.) 2. angry because someone has something that you would like to have (Jim was *jealous* when Dan got a new skateboard.)

L

laughter the sound of laughing (At a funny play, you will hear the *laughter* of many people.)

laundry clothes that need to be washed (Put the dirty sheets with the other *laundry*.)

lizard an animal that is a little like a snake, but with four legs and a thicker body (*Lizards* eat bugs and small animals.)

lonely feeling alone and wishing for a friend (When Jack goes to camp in the summer, Lizzy feels *lonely*.)

M

market a place where food and other things are sold (Please buy some eggs at the *market*.)

medal a thing you get for winning a game or doing a good job (The person who draws the best picture will win a *medal*.)

medicine something that you take to help you get better when you are sick (When I have a bad cold, my mother makes sure I take all my *medicine*.)

mirror a glass you look in to see yourself (In the *mirror*, I could see my own face.)

mobile something that has wires or strings with things hanging from them (Every time the wind blows, my *mobile* turns and spins.)

mongoose a furry animal about two feet long, with a thin face and tail (A *mongoose* can kill snakes.) *pl.* **mongooses**

month a period of time lasting about 4 weeks or 30 days (The year is made up of twelve *months*.)

mouthful enough to fill a mouth (After it had put three nuts into its mouth, the little squirrel had quite a *mouthful*.)

musical about music; having to do with music (The bird's song sounded *musical*.)

O

object a thing that can be seen or touched (Books, rocks, walls, butterflies, and cats are all *objects*.)

office a place where people work (My mom's *office* is on the 34th floor of a very tall building.)

owner someone to whom something belongs (The *owner* of that car must move it out of the way.)

P

palace a very large, beautiful house for a king or queen (The *palace* had 57 rooms.)

palm[1] a kind of tree that grows in warm places (Most *palms* have big leaves at the top.)

palm[2] the inner side of a hand (Place the dime in my *palm*, please.)

parade many people walking together while others watch (The clowns are my favorite part of the *parade*.)

parent a mother or father (My *parents* tell me what time I should come home.)

pencil a tool to write with (That *pencil* has a sharp point.)

perfect with not one thing wrong (If you write a *perfect* paper at school, you get 100 points or an *A*.)

person a man, woman, or child (Were you the last *person* to play with that toy?)

photographer someone who takes pictures with a camera (When I won the race, a *photographer* took my picture.)

pioneer an early settler in a place (There were no towns in the West before the *pioneers* came.)

polish to rub something to make it smooth and shiny (We *polish* our car with wax.)

possible able to be done; able to happen (Is it *possible* to dig to the center of the earth?)

practice the act of doing something again and again because you want to do it better (To ice-skate well, you need a lot of *practice*.)

prairie   a very large piece of land that is flat or rolling, with just a few trees (We could see a long way across the *prairie*.)

prince   the son of a king (The king gave the *prince* anything he wanted.)

principal   someone who runs a school (When the teacher needs something, he asks the *principal*.)

Q

question   what you ask to find something out (Try not to ask your mother too many *questions* when she is busy.)

R

rare   not seen or found very often (There once were a lot of tigers in the jungle, but now they are very *rare*.) **rarer, rarest**

regular   the kind you see most often; not special (Most *regular* school buses are yellow.)

remove   to take away; to get rid of (Please *remove* your toy truck from the chair.)

reply   to say something back; to answer (I called and called to Tom, but he did not *reply*.) **replied, replying**

return   to go back to (After school, we all *return* to our homes.)

roller skate   a shoe with four little wheels on the bottom. It is used for moving around floors or sidewalks. (Carlos glides along on his *roller skates*.)

S

saddlebag   a bag put on a horse for carrying things (The rider took some food out of her *saddlebag*.)

salesperson someone who sells things (When Mr. Dexter walked into the store, the *salesperson* asked if he needed any help.)

scoreboard the board that shows how many points a person or a team has made (The *scoreboard* shows that our team is winning the baseball game, 3 to 1.)

scorecard a piece of paper for marking the number of points that someone makes in a game or contest (During the golf game, Lee marked his *scorecard* after each turn.)

sculptor an artist who makes sculptures (See **sculpture.**) (The *sculptor* made a statue of a bird.)

sculpture a work of art that is carved, molded, or shaped in some way. It is made out of a material such as stone, clay, metal, or wood. (Mike's wooden *sculpture* of a whale won first prize at the school art show.)

search to look for something (Did you have to *search* for a long time to find your pencil?)

settle to stay somewhere new (If we like Texas, we may *settle* in that state.) **settled, settling**

settler someone who makes a home in some new place where few people live (In the old days, many *settlers* moved to the western part of our country to make new homes.)

shudder to shake a little because of fear (Some people *shudder* at just the thought of riding in an airplane.)

skate　to move along on shoes with little wheels or sharp blades on the bottom　(When you *skate*, you seem to glide along.)　**skated, skating**

sorry　sad; wishing you had done something else　(Shari was *sorry* that she forgot her grandmother's birthday.)　**sorrier, sorriest**

strange　different; not like most things　(A green kitten would be a very *strange* sight.)　**stranger, strangest**

supply　an amount of something you want or need, such as food or water　(Dad chopped a *supply* of firewood for the campfire.)　*pl.* **supplies**

swallow　to move food from the mouth into the stomach; to eat　(I watched a bird *swallow* 15 bugs.)

T

terrarium　a glass case to keep plants and pets in　(I can see my turtle in its *terrarium*.)

thousand　ten times one hundred　(A *thousand* balloons would fill up a room.)

ticket　a piece of paper that shows you have paid to go to something like a game, movie, or show　(This *ticket* to the play cost two dollars.)

tiptoe　to walk on the tips of the toes　(You are quieter when you *tiptoe* than when you run.)　**tiptoed, tiptoeing**

tractor　a big machine on wheels, used to pull things such as a plow　(The farmer uses the *tractor* to plow and to pull a wagon.)

transparent　able to be seen through　(The window glass is *transparent*.)

tuna a big fish that lives in the sea and is good to eat (Open a can of *tuna* for lunch.)

u

umpire someone who rules on the plays of a game (The *umpire* said that the player was safe.)

undressed not dressed; having no clothes on (You must get *undressed* before you take a bath.)

v

vibes (short for **vibraphone**) a musical instrument that is like the xylophone (I like to listen to my brother play the *vibes*.)

w

wagon a cart with four wheels used to carry things (Bring the hay to the barn in the *wagon*.)

washtub a large tub for washing clothes or taking a bath (We used the campfire to heat water for the *washtub*.)

weave to put threads together to make cloth (When you *weave*, you make threads go over and under each other.)

weaver someone who makes cloth out of threads or yarn (The *weaver* used red and pink yarn to make this cloth.)

wheel something that is shaped like a circle and turns (Cars have four *wheels*, and bikes have two.)

wonder something strange and surprising (After all the trouble she had, it is a *wonder* that she finished the job.)

Cover/Cluster Openers   Design: Studio Goodwin-Sturges.   Illustration: Holly Berry.   Calligraphy: Colleen.

Editorial   Book Editors: Laura A. Tills, Meg Buckley.   Senior Editor: Susan D. Paro.   Editorial Services: Marianna Frew Palmer, K. Kirschbaum Harvie.   Permissions Editor: Dorothy Burns McLeod.
Design   Series: Leslie Dews.   Book: Mary Keefe, Kathy Reynolds, Ellen Coolidge, Ingrid Cooper.
Production   Mary Hunter.

Illustration   **10–16:** James Marshall, copyright © 1983, from *Fox on Wheels*, with permission. **18–19:** Stephen Moscowitz. **20–24:** Slug Signorino. **26–32:** Cat Bowman Smith. **36–44:** Brinton Turkle. **46–52:** Mary Stevenson Keefe. **54–66:** Phillippe Dupasquier. **70–71:** Laura Cornell. **72–80:** Catherine O'Neil. **82–89:** Alan Daker, border, Nancy Evers. **91:** Dorothea R. Sierra. **92–100:** Catherine Stock. **104–114:** Sandra Speidel. **116–118:** Cyndy Patrick. **120–133:** Bob Shein. **136–147:** Anne Barrow. **149–158:** Dorothea R. Sierra. **170–178:** Judy Love. **180–183:** Reynold Ruffins. **184:** Susan Banta. **186–196:** Allan Eitzen. **207–218:** Marc Brown, copyright © 1979, from *Arthur's Eyes*, with permission. **220–221:** Cecily Lang. **222–231:** Jack Kent, copyright © 1982, from *The Caterpillar and the Polliwog*, with permission. **234–236:** Diana Bryan. **238–246:** Marcia Sewall. **248–256:** Irene Trivas. **258–270:** Jean and Mou-sien Tseng. **272–285:** Jan Pyk.

Photography   **46:** Ashod Francis (Animals Animals). **47:** Jane Burton (Bruce Coleman, Inc.). **48:** © Jeffrey L. Rotman. **49:** Jane Burton (Bruce Coleman, Inc.). **50:** © Jeffrey L. Rotman (Peter Arnold). **51:** Allan Power/National Audubon Society (Photo Researchers). **52:** © Jeffrey L. Rotman. **116–118:** Ken O'Donoghue © D.C. Heath. **149,150:** Pedro E. Guerrero. **151:** *tl,* The Photo Source; *cr,* Collection of the Chase Manhattan Bank. **160,162:** Wide World Photos. **164:** *t,* UPI/Bettmann Newsphotos; *bl,* DEJEAN/SYGMA; *br,* Canapress Photo Service. **165:** Canapress Photo Service. **166:** *bl,* Wide World Photos; *br,* Canapress Photo Service. **200:** *tl,* David R. Frazier; *tr,* Fred Bodin (Stock Boston); *cl,* © Brent Jones; *cr, bl, br,* David R. Frazier; *bc,* Erika Stone. **201:** *tl,* Jim Whitmer; *tc,* Ellis Herwig (Stock Boston); *tr,* Freda Loinwand; *bl,* Victoria Beller-Smith; *br,* Jim Whitmer. **202:** *tl,* Hazel Hankin; *tc,* David R. Frazier; *tr,* Edward Lettau (FPG); *bl,* Freda Loinwand; *br,* Hazel Hankin. **203:** *tl,* David R. Frazier; *tr,* © Lou Jones; *cl,* Victoria Beller-Smith; *c,* Linda Benua; *bl,* Julie Houck; *br,* Gloria Karlson. **204:** *tl,* Dennine Cody (FPG); *tc,* Hazel Hankin; *tr,* Terry E. Eiler (Stock Boston); **204:** *cr,* Jim Whitmer; *bl,* Julie Houck; *br,* Jeffrey W. Myers (FPG). **205:** *tl,* Jean-Claude Lejeune; *tr,* Julie Houck; *cl,* David Phillips; *c,* Aaron Haupt (Frazier Photolibrary); *bl,* Julie Houck; *br,* Norman Prince. **206–207:** Ken O'Donogue © D.C. Heath.
Photo Coordinator: Connie Komack.   Photo Research: Jennifer Ralph.   Photo Styling: Elizabeth Willis, Nanci Lindholm.